Broke In The City

Living a 200K Lifestyle on a 40K Budget

Broke In The City

Living a 200K Lifestyle on a 40K Budget

MAYRA PERDOMO

Broke In The City: Living a 200K Lifestyle on a 40K Budget
By Mayra Perdomo

Published by NY On A Budget LLC

Printed in the United States of America

First Edition: November 2023

ISBN-13: 978-1-962917-01-8

ISBN-10: 1-962917-01-8

DEDICATION

This book is dedicated first and foremost to my mother and grandparents.

They invested in my education, provided a phenomenal upbringing, and taught me to live a balanced life, which resulted in this book.

I also want to thank all my aunts, uncles, cousins, friends and their parents, roommates, teachers, and co-workers. Everything I have learned in my life is a culmination of what I have learned from everyone I have encountered, even those random exchanges of information with strangers.

Thank you.

PREFACE

This is my first book, and I have no clue how to write a preface. I hope you enjoy my feeble efforts in trying to lure you into reading this enticing and engaging composition of privileged information. Please only share with those you deem worthy of acquiring this sacred knowledge.

Now that you get my sense of humor, you are probably wondering what inspired me to write this book?

Well, one of my roommates recommended I write a book on the tips and tricks of budgeting I shared with her. These tips allowed me to travel, dine, and furnish the apartment. In that moment, just like that, the decision to write the book was made. That day, I began writing, actually voice dictating. Having been in a car accident the prior year, my wrist still hurt, so writing was not an option, nor was typing, so voice dictation was the best option. Siri became my assistant. *She* was horrible and should've been fired, but she was free, so I kept her around. It was probably the fourth time someone suggested I write a book, so I took it as a sign from the universe and just did it. It was a very *legally blonde* moment.

Truth be told, I am a walking plethora of information. I love to research and learn, and many people consider me a knowledge seeker. I found that people were always asking me how I acquired the things I had, could afford to go out so often, and travel so much (24 countries and over 125 international cities so far, plus three additional countries, if you count the layovers I left the airport to explore.). When I shared the information with friends, strangers, and family, I found myself sharing my tips and tricks repeatedly. It was very time-consuming. Now, I can direct everyone here to get the information, making sure it reaches the people it could benefit most. I should get paid for my time and knowledge, right?!

Gathering the information was simple since I had already created a Facebook page many years ago called "NY on a Budget" where I list free and inexpensive things to do in the NYC area. It can be found at **www.facebook.com/nyoab.** I referenced many of the posts I had shared in the past. By taking those notes and concepts and morphing them into this book, I was able to create this... Get excited!

I'm sure you are wondering how long it took me to write and publish this magnificent work. Initially, writing this book didn't take long. It took about two weeks to write everything via voice dictation and about four months to edit it using grammarly (don't do that it's not meant for book writing, it actually made it worse for the editor.) Then I had the car accident (you'll read about it later). One year and five months after the car accident I was ready to do this...

Then, the pandemic of 2020 hit, which would have been the best time, however, I had to use my savings to get by and could not afford to self-publish. Oddly enough, this was a blessing, as I was then able to add more information during the pandemic because I was now implementing every tactic I had learned in life to survive it.

When I was finally ready, I paid a recommended colleague $1500 to help me publish the book. I submitted my work to the editor, there were a ton of suggestions that took another few months to revise. Finally, four years after I started writing the book, it was ready to be copyrighted, published, and released, but the editor disappeared. I waited nine months for a response. Crickets. She basically ran away with my money.

One night I decided to do it myself. I spent nine hours trying to figure out how to self publish, registering for different outlets, reformatting the cover, back cover and a few other things and then submitting it. Finally at 5 o'clock in the morning, it was submitted as an e-book and a paperback. Unfortunately there were some typos I missed that have since then been corrected. It took less than a week to correct this.

Now that I understand the process, the next few books should be easier to write and publish. You can do it, too! If you have a great idea, start dictating or taking notes, surely there are people out there who can benefit from your life lessons. If you would like me to walk you through it, you can contact me on a consulting basis or take my course, which inevitably, I will create. That's what people do now, right? www.mayraperdomo.com

Table of Contents

INTRODUCTION

There are so many books on budgeting. When you incorporate those strategies, it becomes extremely time-consuming, and you spend more money *trying* to save money than actually saving money. I tried cutting coupons, making lists, and signing up for websites that resulted in a ton of spam, and I wasn't any better off.

I don't mind spending money, I just want to make sure I get the most for the money I spend. I like to invest in experiences that lead to amazing memories. In the following pages, I will share with you my practices and how I incorporated the methods in this book to create a fantastic life for myself. Hopefully, you can incorporate some of this into your life to make it a little bit more fabulous.

Warning: If you're someone with a type-A personality that gets annoyed with horrible grammar, current vs past tense or colloquial language, sorry in advance. I've chosen to write this book, as if I were speaking to you directly. In the tone of a friend sharing what they've learned. Fun, right?

Why on earth should you read this book or buy it if you're trying to decide to buy it?

Well.... I am guessing it's because you would like to learn how to live a 200k lifestyle on a 40k budget...and laugh a little. Since I'm pretty good at living an extraordinary, semi-luxurious life on the aforementioned budget, I am pretty sure you will benefit from learning how to implement some of the recommendations found throughout the book.

Most of my tips and tricks have been compiled on the following pages with a lot of love, humor, genuineness, and a dash of frankness. Whether you have money, or you're broke, this book will teach you quite a few things. You will find several tips on saving money. If you have money, you will learn how to spend it more efficiently.

On a spiritual and purpose-driven level, I wrote this with the hope it reaches the people it's meant to. Some people may merely find this entertaining while others will find the advice useful. My sincere goal is to reach those who are having difficulty getting by on their current income and could truly benefit from the information in these blessed pages.

Everyone can learn how to live a fabulously frugal lifestyle regardless of economic background. For those who are ever put into a situation where you are struggling financially, especially after this recent pandemic, or you are just looking to save money, this book will give you insight and ideas while helping you save your sanity in the process.

I truly hope you enjoy reading this, if not, at least you'll learn some money-saving/smart spending techniques or get a few good chuckles. More information specific to cutting costs and streamlining businesses and start-ups can be provided on a consulting basis. Bookings for consultations, speaking engagements, and corporate trainings / incubations should be requested at www.mayraperdomo.com.

Disclaimer: Everything written in this book is what I heard or learned. I am not a financial advisor. I am just sharing with you what I have learned throughout my journey. As the laws change, so does some of the information in this book.

I make no income from the companies I mention in this book, so if a representative of any of the companies noted reads this and would like to send me some gift cards or gift codes via email (no links please, I never click links), I would gladly accept them. Thank you. (I love your company.) You can reach me at www.mayraperdomo.com.

If you would like to know about me, continue to Chapter 1: About me, but if you wish to learn how to save money on items you are purchasing and get free stuff, you can skip this chapter and go straight to Chapter 3. So, let's get started.

CHAPTER
One

ABOUT ME

When I first wrote this book, it was a simple guide. There was no humor or information about me. However, when ALL my friends proofread it, they all said I should write more about myself and include more of my personality. With that said, I would like to share with you a little bit about my past, upbringing, career path, and experiences so you can get an idea of who I am and how I obtained the information for this book. I know you bought this book to learn tips and tricks, so I will try to keep it somewhat short.

Family and Upbringing: My grandparents raised eight children who had multiple children each. Providing for that many people is not easy. My grandfather taught his children and us, his grandchildren, to save, find free events that everyone could attend, and take as many gift/marketing handouts that you could, to share with the family, chip in as a family, and most of all, love unconditionally. That's probably why I'm such a giving person.

My grandparents were the pillars of the family and two of my greatest blessings. I was raised by a village, and that village had a significant influence on me as a child. I believe it is essential that a child observe various personalities and identify different ways of doing the same thing to get the same outcome because we all do things differently. This diversity shaped me into the person I am today.

My dad, Rolando Perdomo, tried out for the Yankees and didn't make it when he first arrived in this country. Instead, he became a radio VJ (voice jockey,) RJ (radio jockey) and DJ (disc jockey). He was an outstanding radio personality on two radio stations, WJIT and 97.9 FM in the 70's-80's when it was Radio Hit before it became La Mega. He was a master of ceremony for several occasions in NYC and had his own TV show on Public Access. He was also an auxiliary police officer.

According to a multitude of people, he was super hot and was considered sexy with his amazing radio voice. Everyone crushed on my dad. He taught me to have fun, be joyful, believe in God, read the Bible (which I'm still working on, along with the Torah, Quran, and any other religious texts), and treat everyone with dignity and respect. I was trying to get him to start a podcast in 2021 because he still had that radio voice and so many fascinating experiences and knowledge I thought should be shared. Then, in May 2021, he had a stroke and lost his ability to speak due to aphasia. Sadly he passed away in February 2023.

My mother was the provider, my best friend, and the most fun person in my life. Her name was also Maira (but it was spelled differently). She taught me and gave me the same things my dad did, less the Bible (she threw in 13 years of catholic school instead), and she provided pretty much everything else. She taught me entrepreneurship, diplomacy, work ethic, etiquette, class, and more. She provided me with an excellent upbringing, education, and opportunities. She was friends with diplomats and ambassadors. My mom judged local beauty pageants and was part of the Dominican Council that moved the Dominican Parade to 6th Avenue. She was purely amazing. She was and is one of the most elegant women I have ever seen, and I have seen and met many. I learned (was forced to) to confidently walk into a room and meet and converse with every single person so I would know everyone by the end of the night. Confidence and the ability to network are great gifts to bestow upon your children.

I grew up with my mom running her own business. It was all I knew. So, I knew when I grew up, I would work my way to the top and learn everything I needed to so I could run my own business. I never wanted to climb or stay on the corporate ladder. It was never an option.

My family was considered upper-middle class, and many people thought we were rich. We did not start that way. Like most immigrant families, my grandfather and his children worked hard to create a base for us. When we (my cousins and I) were born as first-generation Americans, we saw the struggle and the rewards. We utilized every resource and opportunity, and as a family, we grew, educated each other, and prospered. Then, inflation hit, and we were fucked like so many other Americans. (Facts: Inflation rose quickly, and the amount of money people made or had saved did not match the inflation rate. Only the people in my family who owned real estate before 2000 maintained a decent lifestyle since they bought when the market was 75% lower than it is now. Those of us paying rent have not been doing so well ever since. Lesson: Invest in real estate. It helps you combat inflation.)

With the excessive increase in property value (did the value really increase?), it's not beneficial to buy in the five boroughs. The Bronx is the last affordable borough. Even if you try to buy something, you are basically a slave to your home for the next 30 years if you can come up with the down payment. Mortgages are so high that if you lose your job, you pretty much lost your house and everything you invested in it. I'd, instead, invest in one to two properties outside of NY and use that rental income to fund a NY property, but I'm not investing everything into one NY property.

While my grandfather was frugal, my mom was anything but that. She was smart, and she saved money, but she preferred a luxurious life full of fun. She was a memory maker—she threw the best parties, gave the best gifts, had the first of everything before it even came out, and we traveled everywhere all the time. So, I saw two very different personalities and chose to straddle the line and live a lifestyle that reflected both upbringings.

My Professional Background: I'm an extremely hard worker and have earned every position I had. I paid all my own bills since I was 15 when my mom made me work. I bought my beeper, cell phone, computer, and phone line to access the computer. I even paid for my prom ticket, dress, and limo; I paid for everything on my own (except clothes and food until I moved out). My mom said I had to get a scholarship because she wasn't paying for college, and she didn't. So, I earned a partial scholarship, a grant, and I took out loans. I was forced to be responsible.

I worked hard. Let's be honest: I worked like a donkey my whole life. I had multiple jobs at the same time. I worked every holiday so I could get overtime or double time. I missed so many birthdays and celebrations because I chose to make more money, and now that I'm older, I realize time is more important than money. People are more important than money. Now I'm choosing to work smarter, not harder, to have more time with the people I love.

I graduated from Pace University with a degree in entrepreneurial management. I started with a major in accounting, then switched to international marketing with a focus on Asian culture (took three years of Japanese). Then, I finally switched again to entrepreneurial management. I'm well-rounded.

Before graduating, I worked in customer service for many high-end retail establishments, including the US Open, and I did payroll for US Airways. After graduating, I worked in various fields. I spent five years working as an outside, cold calling, business to business sales agent (this is where I perfected the "never give up, get up when you're down, make it happen, super joyful" attitude). Then a licensed as an NYS real estate salesperson and NYS notary public. Next, the executive assistant to the VP of Sales for a jewelry company, then the executive / personal assistant to the VP and Global Director of a billion-dollar international entity. After that, the office manager at UBER NYC when they launched in NY. Then a licensed as a NYS life insurance agent. I am currently studying for my securities license now. I then began freelancing - photography, professional organizing, assembling furniture, interior design, professional IKEA Pax closet designer and assembler, mounting TV's, shelves, blinds, anything to a wall, consulting, basic WordPress website development. Now, I am an author and am currently transitioning into being a motivational speaker and making documentaries. I was even an extra in the Grand Central Station flash mob scene in Friends with Benefits with Justin Timberlake and Mila Kunis.

I have had some exciting careers. The one people find most interesting is being an executive/personal assistant to millionaires and billionaires. (The Devil Wears Prada is real.) It allowed me to travel to Switzerland and Beijing for work. I loved it. There came a time when I felt I was working harder than I was being compensated for, at that point, I decided to freelance and work for myself. I took random jobs on TaskRabbit, and my income dropped tremendously, but I knew it would be worth it. It was a struggle, yet I knew, in the long run, I'd be earning more money. I'd have control of my time, and it would be a journey that would make me proud of myself. So, I jumped in feet first—actually, it was a belly flop.

With this new loss of income, I had to learn how to survive in New York. I will share with you how I saved, smartly, spent money when I had it, and how I survived when I didn't.

For the past ten years, the majority of my income has been through Taskrabbit, an on-demand platform that allows a client to hire independent contractors to do a variety of tasks. You can download the app, and if you'd like to, you can find me at **www.https://tr.co/mayra.** If this book does well, you will never be able to hire me on there again, as I would be travelling the world. I'm gunning for a NY Times Best Seller listing! Pray for me.

After a few months on TaskRabbit, I did a task for UBER in Long Island City, NY. They liked me so much they hired me as the Office Manager, TLC Specialist, Payroll Director for drivers, and I assisted the Director of Operations and Community management team as well as onboarding the drivers. That was my introduction to the tech industry and I have learned so much since then. I was there for about a year, then went back to tasking on TaskRabbit where I met so many fascinating and famous people and more people in various tech industries. Fun Fact: I was one of the first seven TaskRabbit Ambassadors in the country responsible for onboarding new taskers and essentially mentoring them as they learned to navigate the platform and being a tasker www.taskrabbit.com/ambassadors I even assisted on a task that was featured on Good Morning America in 2015. I was also featured alongside another tasker in a full-page article for **All You** Magazine in the January 2015 edition. Since then I have been published in several online articles in conjunction with TaskRabbit, pertaining to my expertise or advice as a tasker for corporate/home organization and event planning. I was also the first key speaker at the TaskRabbit Global conference in 2022.

Random Plugin: My all-time favorite celebrity moment was when two men randomly came up to me while I was sitting on the steps outside of an apartment building next to this quaint restaurant in the NYC village. I was waiting for my client, as I was scheduled to mount a TV to their wall via a TaskRabbit task. When a gentleman started chatting with me (we didn't know each other), I engaged in conversation. When there was a pause, I looked over at his friend and realized Cuba Gooding, Jr. was in front of me. I did a double-take and stuttered, and they both laughed. I was flabbergasted. That was the best random moment ever!!!! I love when celebrities do this. His friend said I should join them in the restaurant next door when I was done, and I didn't. That is the biggest regret of my life, so if Cuba Gooding Jr. ever reads this book, I would love to join you and your friend for dinner some time. (Throwing it out into the universe.) So back to the book.

On TaskRabbit my specialties are professional organizing, photography, research, personal assisting, data entry, event planning and more. I made consistent/okay money in these categories, but it wasn't until I switched to furniture assembly and mounting that I was making consistently close to $60-$90 an hour (I did not work every day and I only worked a few hours per day).

You're probably wondering how I know how to assemble furniture and mount things to a wall. Here's the story . . . There was a point where I saw jobs being posted for $60-90 an hour for furniture assembly and mounting, and I wanted in on that. By working less and making more money, I could have more time for myself. Forcing myself to learn a new skill to survive, thrive, and have more time culminated a new profession, and now I teach private lessons on how to assemble furniture and mount various items to a wall you can book me at www.mayraperdomo.com

However, since more people have entered the task rabbit platform, prices have dropped due to more competition and a saturated workforce. Luckily, I still get hired consistently as there is a market for people who prefer to hire women.

Building basic WordPress websites was another endeavor learned by watching YouTube videos for 24 hours. I never made excuses; I always tried to learn and execute something new to earn income. What can I say—I like expensive things, and I like to travel.

If you're wondering how I have time to do all of this, it's simple. I am perpetually single. All that time people spend in relationships, thinking about their boo thing, and planning things with their hunny bunny, I spent on me, learning new things traveling to 24 countries and over 125 international cities and finding various ways to thrive on a budget.

Off-topic (random story, I will do this often throughout the book): While rereading this book before sending it in for editing, I was on the phone with my friend, Latiqua Williams, author of the book, "She Did Single Parenting in Heels," also known for being a hair restoration specialist, motivational speaker, CEO of Exxclusive Hair Inc, and mother of **The Real Tarzann** (look him up on Instagram if you haven't heard of him). She said I should mention this random story as it came up in conversation right before I sent my book to get edited. She believes people may want to know this.

After telling her my book title thoughts, one of which was "Surviving", she proceeded to remind me that when I was "surviving," I had gone to visit her in Miami in August 2019. I had been invited to attend another friend's daughter's surprise 21st birthday party on a boat (she is a performer and prefers not to be named). I happen to be close to the family and am invited to many of their familial gatherings. I was super broke but made enough for the flight. Ironically, Latiqua and the birthday girl have the same birthday, so I invited Latiqua to the boat ride as my guest.

Well, Latiqua pointed out what I think is normal is being on a yacht; it was a VERY large catamaran, in Miami with my friend and her family. The lead singer from 112, who sings the song "Cupid," and his wife attended. My friend and the lead singer both sang their upcoming single for the attendees. To me, it was a normal birthday party. Still, Latiqua, who I brought with me, always points out to me that it's not normal to be on a yacht (it was a very large catamaran), have a celebrity sing, and that I should share the story because the average person does not experience this. She says, "Even when you are broke, your life is fabulous."

I have been blessed with meeting people who include me in their life and welcome me into their experiences. I am extremely grateful for this memory but being a personal assistant to millionaires and billionaires has made me numb to being around celebrities. To me, they are just regular people who do outstanding things. I would like to meet Oprah, though.

CHAPTER Two

THE SITUATION & THE SOLUTION

In life situations happen. Instead of focusing on the problem, focusing on the solution will yield you far better results. Seeking solutions to difficult *situations* is, of course, one of the most important tools in surviving the rat race. Providing simple solutions to life's most complicated situations can alleviate stress and create a peace in your mind that is priceless.

What is the situation that brought you to this book?
Did you lose your job, get a divorce, been in an accident, and Worker's Compensation or No-Fault insurance is not compensating you enough for lost wages? Are you just a victim of economic disparity (aka the f'ed up system), or are you still suffering from the pandemic? Perhaps you've gone through a divorce and don't have the income that you used to have or are a single parent just trying to get by. Maybe you are just trying to save some money for retirement, a nice vacation, or you just can't keep up with inflation. If you are like me, you may just be curious and like to read a wide variety of genres, and this intrigued you. Or, you just bought this book because you are my friend. There are many scenarios that may have occurred that brought you here, regardless of the situation…

Welcome!!!!!

Universal situation: Inflation: Although I reside in Queens, New York, many of the tips and tricks shared here can be utilized in many cities in the United States and possibly anywhere in the world.

Living in New York is not easy. Many people have a side gig, multiple jobs, or something they do to earn income. For many, surviving on one income is difficult if not nearly impossible due to inflation, so if you are in a relationship and have someone to share the burden with, be grateful.

Unexpected inflation (the consistent rising cost of items and real estate) tends to hurt those whose wages do not rise with the current inflation rates. I have found that if you take the income most people currently make in NYC and move outside of NYC, you would probably live very comfortably. Still, the way things are presently, to thrive in New York City is not as easy as it was in the 1980s; right now (2021), it is crazy-expensive.

Possible Solution:
Counteract inflation by utilizing your money differently, investing in yourself to increase your income, invest to get returns, get a side hustle, save money where you can and get stuff for free, so you do not have to spend your own money. In this book, you're going to find multiple ways to save money, make money, increase your earnings, or just survive when you're broke. There are various things someone may need daily, and when our income reduces or disappears, it is difficult to survive. Some people may be reading this and not have financial issues; they may just be frugal or just like saving money. There are various tips and tricks you may benefit from as well.

I'm going to share with how I survive (and keep my sanity) whether I have money or not. You will learn how I dealt with the chaos, and hopefully, this will also help some people maintain their sanity through their personal "situation." Thankfully, through the emotional support of friends and family, I was able to get by.

My personal situation: In March 2018, I was involved in a car accident where I was rear-ended, I had to have four surgeries and was unable to work for eight months! In that time I had depleted my life savings, which was essentially my down-payment for a home and had to take out two loans to help me stay afloat. If it weren't for that, I would probably be homeless right now. So, as Suzie Orman says, make sure you have an emergency fund of eight months' worth of income.

Prior to the accident, I was building my business, getting ready to film a docuseries www.theindigenousdocumentary.com, and it was supposed to be my most successful year. I would've earned double what I made the previous year and grown from there, but the car accident halted everything and I lost all that progress and income. It took a toll on my body, mind, and spirit. I pummeled through my life savings, and I was broke - actually I was negative because I owed money. (You know what I mean if you know anything about how insufficient funds piggyback off each other and create the financially destructive cycle that keeps you in a hole like crabs in a bucket. A detailed description of this vicious cycle is detailed in Chapter 9 in The Curse of the Overdraft Fees section. Well, that's what happened to me). I was not doing well.

My personal solution: So, what do you do when you literally have no money? Keep reading . . .

CHAPTER Three

NETWORKING

Networking is crucial to maintain a $200k lifestyle. You can network to make friends, business contacts, find a new career, or feed your soul. The best part is you can network to acquire access to items you may not be able to afford or prefer not to purchase. Tim Ferris mentions in his book, *The 4-Hour Workweek,* you do not need to have the assets to enjoy the lifestyle. If you can meet others who have international properties, boats, etc., you can barter your services for use of their assets. You can stay at a friend's house in the Hamptons or stay on their boat off the coast of Monaco if you maintain great relationships with people who have those assets.

Networking is also a great way to meet people who can aid you in your journey through life. Whether they offer emotional, financial, or spiritual support, maintaining relationships with others can help you a great deal at different points in life.

FIND YOUR TRIBE

The first thing you need to do to survive emotionally is to make sure you have a great network of people around you who love you, care about you and are willing to help you when times are rough. You must also be willing to help them as well. (Thank you, Martin, Michelle, Stephanie, Lila, Derrek, Carmen, Ricky, Ashley, Mom, and Dad.)

When you are suffering, put your pride in your pocket, and reach out to all the people around you. People who make you laugh are the best as it uplifts the soul.

I've always earned and worked for everything I had, and I never asked anybody for money (unless I was paying it back within three days) because I'm not a fan of that awkward moment where someone gives you an excuse of why they can't lend it to you. I've also learned to be careful who you lend money to as they may never pay you back. (Bronx Tale) I quickly learned who I could and could not rely on. You may never realize this until a tragedy occurs.

Side note: I have to mention this quote. I don't know who wrote it, but when looking online, I saw Nipsey Hussle say it several times. This quote has changed my life:

"If you look at the people in your circle and you don't get inspired, then you don't have a circle. You have a cage."

Some people suck the life and money out of you. They keep you in that cage. The cage could represent your peers (if you need them or they need you), drama dynamics, constant negativity, complaining all the time, not believing in you, trying to change your path, verbally or physically abusing you, manipulating you, lying, taking advantage of you, and so many other possibilities. Then there are people who help you, uplift you, encourage you, believe in you, cover the bill sometimes, compliment you, teach you, welcome you, invite you, acknowledge you, edify you, visit you when you're sick, love you, and more. Spend more time with those people.

Network for Business

Your tribe can also consist of a networking business tribe that advises you financially, emotionally, or spiritually. Mentors are fantastic and are highly recommended. They choose you.

There are many free events you can register for to meet people that can help get you in the door (if you are looking for employment or a career change). Sometimes you can eat and drink for free! Yeah, some events provide an open bar or one free drink, others have free food, and some have both or none. When they offer free food or drink, I'm there. Bonus!!!!

Look online for **free networking events** in your zip code or city. Many cities have local business networking events. You can find work here if you impress, converse, and share that you are on the market. You may want to bring a resume and business cards.

Networking may also aid in changing careers. Meeting and keeping in touch with people in different fields allows you to learn of openings in those fields. If you left a good impression and people know you are looking for a career change or employment, they may reach out when they hear of a position opening for which you may be qualified. Networking can open many doors.

Network to Socialize

We all have different likes and dislikes, so it's comforting to find someone to share your interests.

Meeting like-minded people with similar interests can fulfill you on a mental and spiritual level. You can meet people by looking for free meetups, meetings, events, and groups that you can join or can participate in to find like-minded peers.

Meeting people who have more assets, knowledge, power, or influence than you can be useful in that they can teach you how to acquire those resources for yourself. Many people are willing to share and teach others that are open to being students. Others are generous and may let you use their properties when they are not in use. Keep in mind some people may make you pay a fee to stay at their properties, but it is usually less than what you would pay for an Airbnb.

I find many of my friends have difficulty meeting people as they are still trying to adjust to parenting. I strongly recommend (as I learned through friends) if you are a single parent to find a group with other parents where you can set playdates, participate in activities, or meet other parents who agree to watch each other's children which will allow you to have some free time to yourself. It's not easy to find someone that you trust with your children, but at least you're increasing the probability of finding someone that you can.

There are also free programs that will help you find daycare, babysitters, and various services if you seek them. You can search for these programs online; all programs vary depending on city and state.

CHAPTER
Four

THERE IS FREE STUFF EVERYWHERE

There are a multitude of ways to receive free items. In this chapter I have listed the ways I attend free concerts, events, acquire free furniture and items, and even watch movies for free. There is free stuff everywhere if you look for it.

The quickest way to find free stuff is by searching for it online. You can always search the word **free** and then your ZIP Code or the city and state you live in. If you want to be more specific, you can type **free entertainment, free food, free clothes, free tools,** etc. Be careful of any free promotions that request you go online and enter too much information. I don't recommend that (unless it's a radio station promotion).

Then there are more niche ways of finding things. I have listed a few of my favorite freebies below with a brief description on how to get them.

CONCERTS (I love concerts.)

Check out **ilovefreeconcerts.com** They send emails to let you know what concerts are free and how to register for the tickets. They even have contests you can enter to win free tickets for various events.

CRAIGSLIST.ORG TICKET SECTION

Sometimes people are giving away tickets in the free or ticket section on Craigslist. You can type the name of a concert or artist in the search box of that section, and you can find people giving tickets away because they cannot attend the concert. Sometimes theaters give away tickets to fill up the venue. You can just pick up the tickets at the will call window of the venue after reserving your tickets by replying to the Craigslist post and receiving a confirmation.

When people are giving away their personal tickets, they may meet with you in person or transfer them to your Ticketmaster or Livenation account or send you their email confirmation. I have received one to four tickets to see a range of performances from great indie productions to opera and ballet tickets at Lincoln Center to art gallery showings. You never know what you can find until you look. Please note the ticket section is different from the free section on Craigslist.

If there are no free tickets, you can still get them at a fraction of the price because the original ticket holder can no longer attend the event and would generally like to recoup some funds before they lose everything. I strongly suggest you only purchase tickets from someone you meet in person (I always take a picture of them stealthily, never obviously, in case they sell me fake tickets so I can report it to the police, but that's never happened).

Also, be careful of sending money via PayPal or Venmo first, and then having the tickets transferred to you. That's usually a sign of a scam. I prefer to meet someone and have them transfer the tickets via Ticketmaster or Live Nation in front of me as I pay them.

Craigslist Free for Home Items

On www.Craigslist.org there is a **For Sale** section. Under that section, there's a category called **Free**. That's all the stuff people are giving away for free in your area!

Many people give away great furniture because they're moving. When rednovating any part of my apartment, I go on the **Craigslist.org** free section, and look for people who are giving away stuff for free.

Finding wood furniture that can be painted is preferred over particle board as it lasts longer and it tends to look and age better, and you can resell it, so it's an excellent investment. As for electronics, be careful. I would not buy refurbished electronics items like a cell phone or computer from a third-party seller (it's OK to purchase it directly from the manufacturer). Some people put spying software on laptops and phones and resell them cheaply so that they can get your personal information and passwords. Old electronics like cd players, DVD players, an air purifier, etc., are OK. Devices where you input your personal information and passwords? Absolutely not.

Also, bugs and bug eggs can live in electronic devices, so if you go to someone's house and see roaches, don't take anything unless it doesn't bother you.

Dumpster Diving / Garbage Day Searching

You're not going to believe this, but wealthy people throw out the best furniture, and many times there's nothing wrong with it; they're just redecorating. Not to mention they sometimes throw out brand new super expensive clothes with the tags still on them. (Those are great to sell on eBay.) So, on garbage day, you can drive through with a truck and pick up whatever you like.

Check for damages and bugs because you never know. If it doesn't match your decor, but you like it, paint it or sell it. Beautiful furniture is costly and hard to find.

If you are understandably uncomfortable about taking furniture from the garbage, there are people on Craigslist, OfferUp, Letgo, eBay, and other sites selling their household items because they're getting something new. They tend to sell them at affordable prices, and you can usually negotiate/haggle.

Searching through garbage is illegal in some states and counties. Check your local laws before attempting this. If you're in Manhattan and your dumpster diving, It's best to do this in the winter when it's really cold because there's less chance of a bed bug infestation as the cold kills the bugs. If it's freezing, I leave stuff outside or in the car overnight to be safe before bringing it into my home. In the summer, you have to be careful because that's when bugs thrive.

If you live in an apartment building, you can ask your super or doorman if anybody is throwing a specific type of furniture out and, if they are, if you can view it before they throw it on the street. You have to leave your number behind, and you may find what you're looking for, or you may acquire a stalker (maybe use a Google number and be careful.)

If you live in a building, tell your super what you're going to throw out, and maybe somebody else will want it. The super is like the gossip column for your building. I honestly believe the supers in apartment buildings should take furniture left in the garbage room and let other tenants come and take it if they want it. They could also call the Salvation Army (because I know they do pick-ups), or a charity of choice can come to pick it up, so it doesn't go to waste. Side note: The Salvation Army sometimes doesn't show up even if you have an appointment, and they cherry-pick; they don't take everything.

You can also list it on Craigslist.org's free section or on mobile apps like OfferUp, Letgo, etc. If you have a home, some people will put the item outside and do a curb alert posting on Craigslist.org's free section so whoever is in the area can pick it up.

My neighbors threw out a leather couch, and my ex-boyfriend asked if we could have it. We sold it on Craigslist.org the same day for $300. That helped us with rent.

ENTERTAINMENT

There are tons of free events in every city. Look online for **free events** in your area. You can search the term "**free events**" with the name of your town or ZIP Code. You can also search for **free concerts, free festivals, free shows, free activities,** etc. As mentioned earlier, they may list movie showings in parks, classes in libraries, and networking events. Street fairs are always fun. Most cities have a variety of free events you can participate in.

My grandfather had eight kids, so the only way they could go out was to attend free concerts, shows, and events as a family. This motivated me to start a website, which turned into a Facebook page called **NYonaBudget.com** (or the Facebook page is **www.facebook.com/nyoab)**, where I list many affordable and free events in the NYC area. I'm thinking of starting a food blog and adding it to the website so check it out when you have time!

EXPOS *

There are large events in most states called expos. You can type in **free expo** and then your state or city, and you can register to attend these events. Not only do you gain knowledge and can network, but the expo participants give away tons of free stuff. You can get food samples, office supplies, and more, depending on the expo's theme. I remember I went to the first Cannabis Expo in New York City and learned so much about that industry.

Food expos are my favorite because you get to try samples of various foods. Business and international expos have a lot of free classes that you can take to learn a multitude of things, and you have the opportunity to talk to each business and learn about what they do. You might even find a job if you inquire if they are hiring. Bring a resume and/or business cards.

Job expos tend to give out office supplies, hand sanitizers, and tissues. The main benefit of attending the expo is finding a job and/or seeing what career options are available.

Global Citizen Festival Concert

You can earn free tickets to the annual Global Citizen Concert by subscribing to the app and then completing calls to action which include tweeting, signing petitions, emailing people using the provided template, or taking quizzes. You are considered a Global Citizen when you participate in the calls to actions.

By completing challenges throughout the year, you earn points you could use to enter raffles for concerts and events. If you submit and win, you will earn free tickets. There are many A-list performers who donate tickets to the Global Citizen cause as a thank you for participating in Global Citizen's efforts in trying to make and implement change.

Government-sponsored functions or events

I don't know about other states or cities, but I know in New York, there are always government-sponsored functions and events. You can go to your state or city's online page. If you're not sure how to do that, you can type in a search engine of your choice your city or county, and state, and then type a space and .GOV (ex. Free events Queens New York .gov), and you can find many pages that have information on free business services, activities, computer classes, educational classes, and events.

Libraries also have a lot of events. Many of the libraries where I live in Queens teach computer basics to people who don't know how to use Microsoft or a computer. They also have musical artists come in to speak and perform. Sometimes you can participate in a meet and greet with the artist. I'm not sure what may be available near you, but this information may be beneficial for you if you're in another state and reading this book.

Grow your own Food

This requires minimal investment. You can get pots at the Dollar Tree or Home Depot and then some potting soil. You will have to refresh your soil every year with vitamins. But you can grow your own spices and vegetables. If you have a home or backyard, you can plant fruit trees outside and various vegetables.

If you're in an apartment building, you can just place it near the window, or if you have a large ledge, you can place it on the ledge. A lot of people with fire escapes put it on the fire escape. I have heard of neighbors and squirrels going down the fire escape and stealing fruits and vegetables, but it's the risk you take. If that's happening, they probably need it more than you do. I also think it's a fire hazard to put things on the fire escape as it blocks the passage, but people still do it.

I knew someone that created a community garden right outside of their building in the projects. They just started planting spices and underground vegetables in the bushes right in front of their building. And when they were ready to harvest, nobody noticed because they were under or behind the bushes. Nature watered it for them via the rain. After a while, she told a few people, and they started doing the same thing and growing different items, and they would just go to each other's gardens and pick what they needed when they needed it.

Growing spices is easy and very useful if you cook. If you have a window, you can get a small pot that fits on the ledge, fill it with soil and add some seeds. They will grow quickly all year round. Cilantro, basil, oregano, mint, and thyme are just a few spices that grow very quickly. You can either use them fresh or dry them out and then grind them and use them as dried spices.

If you get a larger pot, you can grow green peppers, tomatoes, and a variety of other vegetables. If you're into holistic healing, you can grow aloe plants, and they grow and multiply into separate aloe plants called pups, and you can pull those out and put those into individual pots.

I suggest buying non-GMO seeds and keeping the seeds from the food you eat to replant. Talking to your plants will make them grow faster. The first few harvests you paid for because you purchased all the items, but afterward, it's pretty much free, and you continuously have free food at your fingertips.

Movie Screenings

There are so many websites offering free movie screenings. You get to see the movie before it comes out, and then you just take a survey of what you thought about it. The movie company takes that information and makes any necessary edits. To find websites that offer free screenings, type into the search bar of your preferred search engine online "free movie screening" and then your city and state. You can then sign up for those websites, and they'll send you invitations to upcoming movies. You need to register that you will be attending, and most of the time, it is still first-come, first-serve, so you are not guaranteed a seat. It is always a great way to watch a movie before it comes out for free.

Kayaking

On certain days and times in NYC, they offer free 20-minute kayaking sessions in the summer. Look it up as you may have to register. They may also provide other free activities.

Radio Station Giveaways

I've won concert tickets at least four or five times just by calling in or signing up online for contests and giveaways. I have never won vacations or money, but you may if you try.

Referral Program Bonuses

These are bonuses you get from referring people. So, if you're part of a rewards program, sometimes, if you refer people to join the rewards program and they join, you get free money, credits, or VIP dollars to use toward future purchases. That's free money.

There are people who make a living off of this by posting ads on different forums saying that you can get x amount of dollars off if you use this code. Then, every time somebody uses the code, they earn x amount of dollars. I also know people who have a tree of friends; this is a list of people who contact each other in a specific, agreed-upon order. So, they decide when someone gets a code, they send it down the designated tree, and they all earn a referral.

Taxes

There are programs that many cities offer that prepare your taxes for free if your income is under a certain amount. You have to look up locations and qualifications in your area (you can do this online) to see if you qualify. They are usually located at a library, but since libraries and bookstores are diminishing, they may be located elsewhere.

Travel

Listed below are a few ways to earn free travel.

Timeshare Presentation: First is the infamous timeshare presentation. They lure you in by giving you a free trip. Sometimes it really is a free trip, and sometimes you have to pay the taxes on the hotel, the cruise, airlines, or whatever it is they're offering for "free." These presentations are convincing. I know way too many people who get sucked into these things and end up buying a timeshare. They end up paying annual fees every year, even if they don't use it. If you happen to purchase a timeshare, the timeshare company may come after you by reporting any nonpayment to the credit bureaus, which can damage your credit.

In most cases, you're bound to the contract until the day you die. Other programs only charge an annual maintenance fee only for the years you use, which makes more sense. Either way, this is a great way to get a free trip since all you have to do is sit in a one-and-a-half to three-hour presentation where they try to sell you a timeshare.

Travel Miles:

Someone recently asked me the best way to get the most miles. Basically, you have to choose an airline you love and get their credit cards. If you have excellent credit, you can get multiple credit cards for numerous airlines. I know currently Chase works with United, and Citibank works with American Airlines. Every time you use the card you earn miles. Credit card companies will often give you bonus miles just for signing up or getting approved, or they'll give you additional miles if you meet certain criteria like spending a certain amount within a specific timeframe. Afterward, you just accrue miles for every purchase that you make.

Travel Engines:

When you book through a travel engine like Expedia, Orbitz, Priceline, TripAdvisor, Travelocity, etc., play around to see what the best prices are at the time. Keep in mind all of those companies are owned by two companies, so there's not a lot of play with the price, but you just choose the one that you feel is reliable or that gives you the most points.

Lastly, create an account with several airlines to directly earn miles. So, when you use your credit card (that earns miles from the credit card purchase) on a travel search engine that earns points when you book through the search engine (to use towards discounts on future bookings), plus use the miles you earn directly from the airlines for having a rewards account with them, you earn bonuses three times.

If you don't enter your airline mileage number on the travel search engine, you could contact the airline after your flight, or you can call them before and give them your airline mileage number to link with the ticket number/booking number, so you do not miss out on those miles.

The best part is you don't have to use those airline reward program miles to travel; you could buy items offered through the airline mileage redemption program, including hotel stays, electronics, gift cards, and more. If you have friends with less than 1000 miles earned, you can ask them to transfer their miles to you because they can't do much with 1000 miles, but if you accrue enough miles, you can get a free trip, or you can buy an iPad or something. I always go for gift cards.

Lastly, many of these airlines' mileage reward programs have partner companies that they work with. So even if you're booking an international trip, you can find out which partner company works with your airline. After you've completed the trip, you can contact your airline mileage reward program, give them the confirmation code on your ticket (keep the ticket), and they will transfer those miles from the international partner airline into your airlines' mileage reward account because they have an alliance. So, you can look up travel alliances to see which airlines work with the airlines you have an account with.

CHAPTER *Five*

THE ART OF BUYING SECONDHAND ITEMS

Buying secondhand items can save you quite a bit of money especially when purchasing luxury items. There are many benefits to buying secondhand items; you just have to be careful of bugs. Yep, that's a real concern, not usually with luxury items, but more so with furniture and toys.

Secondhand items have been a staple in all walks of life. Super wealthy people that live in castles are in second-hand homes. I'm sure that home has been inhabited several times over. Those Louis the 14th desks, mirrors, and various vintage furniture have passed through multiple hands. People want quality pieces that are no longer being produced. Since they don't make them anymore, they get passed on from family to family, auction house to auction house, but they're all still secondhand items. They may get retouched or refinished, but there are still secondhand items, especially art, so there's no shame in buying a second-hand item. It just depends on the value that you give it.

If you're looking for high-end secondhand items, you might want to check out therealreal.com, rebag.com,1stDibs.com, StaziaLoren.com <— I helped her for a few weeks when she was first putting the company together.

If you are looking for moderately priced items, Craigslist, Offer Up, and Letgo have great things.

Cars

Get ready for this one. So, I went to school for accounting before changing my major twice. I learned that a car depreciates the moment it's pulled off the lot. My accounting teacher told me it is not a wise investment to lease a vehicle unless you have a lot of money to spend or if you're trying to get a write-off because you make too much money. I have yet to be in either situation, so I buy all my cars on Craigslist.org. I said it: Craigslist. On www.Craigslist.org there is a section called **for sale**. Within that section is a section called **cars+trucks**. That's where I look.

Now, I've been fortunate that I haven't purchased any lemons. I have very low expectations and only expect to use the vehicle anywhere from one to two years. If I get more than that, it's a bonus! I have no problem buying a new car every two years for anywhere from $500-$1,500 instead of leasing a vehicle and spending $1,800-$6,000 a year ($3,600-$12,000 for two years) then having to give it back. After two years, I can sell it or junk it and get some money back.

I get older models that are in good condition with one owner. I try to find vehicles with low mileage, but I'm OKAY with high mileage if it's in excellent condition interior- and exterior-wise. I prefer older cars because they're still made of metal (not fiberglass), and the insurance is very affordable. I don't recommend full coverage unless the blue book value is worth it. I only get liability which saves me a lot of money. Think about it: if you get full coverage and the blue book value is $600-$1500, you're basically giving the insurance company your money. For that amount, you're better off just buying another car. It's not worth paying the extra money in full coverage for these older vehicles.

Luckily the 1997 Ford Explorer saved me when I was in a car accident. This car literally saved me from more physical harm than I am currently in because it took a good hit. It had a real metal bumper, and I was hit so hard that my hitch was stuck in the other car. Their entire front end of the other vehicle was smooshed (it was totaled). It took them an hour to pull the cars apart. They had to pull the other car up into a vertical position with the tow truck so that the police officer could drive my car away. It took what felt like 10 minutes to get the car unstuck. I thought my tires were going to go bald or that I would get a flat because the tires kept spinning, and the cars would not separate.

My priority is not having a fancy or beautiful car; it's in having one that works. You can get a fancy or beautiful car if you want one, but I don't think it's essential at this stage in my life. If I had a car that was made with fiberglass, the car would have been completely crushed, and I'm pretty sure the impact would have caused more permanent damage to my body than I already have from the accident because I would have felt it a lot more. So yeah, I prefer older vehicles that were made from 1997 to 2003, but that's just my preference.

I like anything Volvo. Their heated seats and attention to detail are impeccable. From the quality of the leather to the stitching, to all the functions they seamlessly integrate into the vehicle. I love them. I also really like the Ford Explorer XLT for the height and space. The best part of buying a used car every two years is driving different cars and experiencing multiple brands and vehicle types to gauge which vehicle I might want to buy in the future. I've had several European cars and some American brands, from sedans and SUVs to station wagons. I just got a Volvo Station Wagon and I love it!

(Ironically enough, after I sent this book in for editing, I bought a lemon. I sold the Volvo and Ford when I left to film my documentary www.theindigenousdocumentary.com I thought I would be gone for 6 months and did not need to pay car insurance for 2 vehicles for 6 months. Unfortunately, I returned after a month to care of my father who suffered a terrible speech impairing stroke. I paid 2k for a Lexus crossover and I had to put 3.5k in to fix it but it's perfect now. I will probably end up giving this to my little brother when he gets his license as it's a great car. Prior to this moment I never had any issues. This seller was upset when I turned the car off, this is a surefire way to know they have cleared the codes and there are probably issues. Also, he was pressuring me to buy it by using fear of loss saying things like "If you don't want it I have a bunch of people that do, so let me know." Be wary of these tactics.

Car Parts

Junkyards are great because you don't have to spend a lot of money on new parts. It's important to check with your local junkyard to see what kind of parts are commonly stocked prior to purchasing a vehicle. I prefer to buy a vehicle that I know they will have plenty of parts for. I've learned it's expensive to buy a vehicle that will cost a lot to repair, like Volvo, BMW, or Mercedes.

I don't mind buying used parts because I already know this is a short-term investment. I'm looking to get one to two years out of the car and then junk it and get some money back for the next vehicle. You get more money back when the original parts are in a vehicle. I always try to buy a car with one owner and low mileage if possible with no issues and haven't had any problems yet. If you get a lemon, don't get mad at me.

There is a town or a place where you have considerably inexpensive car parts in almost every state. I'm from Queens, New York, so it used to be the area across from Shea Stadium (now Citifield) until the city used eminent domain (the taking of private property for the public good while fairly compensating the owners) to take over the land. They are currently tearing down the businesses to build co-ops and condos. Now, the place to get car parts is Boston Rd. in the Bronx. I know down south they have "Pick a Part" locations where you physically pick your piece and take it out of the vehicle. Those places tend to be extremely affordable.

Another great place to buy parts is eBay. Many of these parts are manufactured and sent from Korea or China, but they work and are significantly cheaper. Ask your mechanic the cost for parts and labor. If you can find the parts cheaper than what the mechanic quotes, let them know you'll bring your own parts in. It tends to be a lot more affordable to do that. Now keep in mind if you do that, the mechanic doesn't generally guarantee the parts; they only guarantee the labor, which means if anything goes wrong, they tend to blame the part. I haven't had that happen yet, but they always tell me that.

Clearly, if I'm buying a car for $600 and something occurs that costs more than $150-$350 to fix, I'll just buy another car for $600. I never pay more in repairs than I paid for the car. I'd rather make a short-term, one-time, low-cost investment than a high-cost investment because the girl who hit me totaled her car, and it was a brand new 2017 car which was leased, and this accident happened in March 2018.

I asked my mechanic what happens if you get into an accident with a lease, and I was told (hearsay) you have to pay off the remainder of the lease even though the car was totaled. I believe insurance may cover that, but if you want a new lease, there's an additional charge to it, and obviously, your insurance goes up because that's a high replacement cost as opposed to my Kelley Blue Book value of $1200.

CRAIGSLIST.ORG

People are continually getting rid of their lightly used items. You can buy them under the sale section on the Craigslist.org page for your city, or you can find them under the free section on Craigslist.org in the sale section.

I bought both of my Nespresso machines for under $30 on Craigslist! Those things are crazy expensive. When people come over, and I serve them Nespresso coffee, they think I'm so chic. They have no idea I paid $30 for the machine. Well, now they do, but they would've never known before.

I found the best prices for the coffee pods are on Amazon, Walmart, and eBay. If you know a better site to get genuine Nespresso coffee pods cheaper, let me know. The best prices I found to date were on Amazon for the Vertuo coffee pods and eBay or Walmart for the classic line. However, if you have Amazon Prime you tend to receive the items much quicker than on eBay.

You can get a Vitamix, waffle irons, blenders, Ninjas, etc.--anything you need for your kitchen that's pretty expensive you can buy inexpensively in your local neighborhood via Craigslist.org. The best part is getting to go and test it when you pick it up and decide whether you want it after viewing it. This is also a great option for TVs. If you're trying to get a good deal on a TV, sometimes you get a 40- or 50-inch TV relatively cheap because they bought a bigger TV and no longer have use for the one they are selling.

Side note: I would stay away from secondhand Dyson products. People tend to sell the Dyson products because they lose suction or don't blow cool or hot air as effectively.

You can buy bed frames, headboards, and even mattresses on Craigslist.org. You might not want to hear this, but I've never purchased a brand-new mattress. I always acquired my mattress and bed frames for free on Craigslist under the free section. I always look for someone that was here for schooling and was going back home and needed to get rid of the mattress and bed frame. I've brought home some amazing, crazy- expensive mattresses for free. Always buy a full zippered allergen mattress cover (one that protects from bed bugs is ideal) to use on the bed and another for the box spring.

Now that I'm older, when I buy an apartment or house, I would like to purchase a brand-new mattress and bed frame. But in my 20s and 30s, I didn't care.

I rent a three-bedroom apartment, and I have two roommates. I usually furnish their rooms and acquire the furnishings for free on Craigslist. This is a great option if you have children, and you need to furnish their rooms on a limited budget.

If you are not into secondhand mattresses, but it's time for a new bed, you might want to consider a foam mattress topper. You can buy them for under $100 on Amazon or various other websites. It will upgrade your bed for anywhere from six months to two years. You can also buy a foam topper to see how you feel about a foam bed. It is a great way to avoid buying a new bed for a year or two. I recommend 4" foam toppers if you like it a bit firm, or if you like it super soft, add a pillow top topper.

Estate / Garage / Yard Sales

I love these!!! When I was a kid, my aunt and my mom dragged me to all of these garage sales. As I got older, we went to estate sales (these are excellent for antique furniture and jewelry). They tried to teach me how to haggle, which I don't do. It's either a fair price or not--I'm not going to argue with someone to try and get a lower price.

My aunt, on the other hand, does not budge. If he said it was "$10," she would reply, "One dollar." If they would say, "Five dollars," she would reply, "One dollar." Then, she would giggle and take it, whenever they said a price she thought was fair. Her ideology is they want to get rid of it; they will throw it out at the end of the day, so give it to me for a dollar. LOL. I love her. Even if it was $100, she would say, "One dollar."

I purchased some of the most memorable items I have ever had and still have several items I purchased at garage sales. I bought a Louis Vuitton and Gucci purse 30 years ago for two dollars because the lady thought I was cute. She had no idea I knew what it was. Back then, there was no internet, or high-end, secondhand stores. Goodwill and Salvation Army were the only thrift shops, and they were not cool, so there was no other way to sell it, so people sold it for whatever. (I had that bag for about 15 years, then I brought it to Gucci to get fixed, and then I sold it.) I also bought a Louis Vuitton Sac Plat for five dollars. I still have it 30 years later.

There are treasures everywhere. Some people do not know how to use the internet and sell great finds at garage sales, so keep an eye out. I've found great photography items, kitchen items, comic books, and records, which I love! It's a great way to get what you need at an affordable rate.

Quick story: A lady across the street was selling 15 sets of gorgeous china since her mother-in-law passed and they were hers. On the last day she just started giving stuff away for free since they were selling the house and weren't keeping anything. I was given two of the most unique sets of china that I use every year for my potluck dinner--for free!

There are people who go back on the last day to make their final offer or see if they can get something significantly lower than the original asking price. Then there are people who wait until everything gets thrown out and they go through the garbage to get things for free. Yep.

Government Auctions

Almost all governments / counties / cities have auctions for the seized items. Whether it's real estate, cars, or a variety of different things, you can go to these auctions and bid. If you win, you must pay the full amount at the end of the day. Look up government auctions in your area

Sharing or Gifting

So, karma is real. If you give something to someone in need, it will come back to you when you need something.

Instead of disposing and throwing away items, it's best to donate them or pay it forward. What I normally do is I take whatever I don't need and put it in a bag and give it to the next homeless person I see. Whether it's half a tube of toothpaste, a quarter bottle of shampoo, conditioner, or lotion, they can benefit from all these things. If a homeless person refuses your products, do not get offended. They may have allergies to some items and do not feel they need to discuss it.

When I travel, I always grab all the travel-size shampoo, conditioner, soap, and complimentary toiletries from the hotel and the toiletry bag from the flight, put them together, and I give them to the next homeless person I see.

Some of my high-end clients keep the high-end toiletries and put them in a small basket with a towel and washcloth for guests.

Swap parties

It's not what you think. Basically, what you do is you get together, and you grab all the stuff you no longer want. Then you meet up with your friends and they bring the stuff that they don't want. Then you lay everything on the table, and for every one piece that you put down, you take a piece. So, you guys are swapping your stuff. Instead of going out and buying things, you can just get it from friends or acquaintances. It's good to have a theme. You can choose the theme or a few themes.

Here are a few themes, and keep in mind themes can be combined:

- ☐ Jewelry
- ☐ Handbags
- ☐ Hiking / camping gear
- ☐ Kitchen items
- ☐ Toiletry items
- ☐ Office supplies
- ☐ School supplies
- ☐ Shoes
- ☐ Clothes
- ☐ Baby items
- ☐ Toys
- ☐ Kids clothes
- ☐ Home decor
- ☐ Perfumes
- ☐ Electronics
- ☐ Food, etc.

You can get creative.

CHAPTER
Six

DIY / REPURPOSING - YOU CAN DO IT

There are so many ways to repurpose things and so many things you can do yourself. I highly recommend looking these up. I'm only going to list a few things I suggest trying, but if you search online, you can get lost for hours on DIY and repurposing articles and videos.

REPURPOSING

Sometimes it's better to repurpose something than to throw it out or get rid of it. Everything can have a second life if you shift how you look at its purpose. Below are a few of my favorites. You can also look up repurposing online to get some more ideas.

I took a hanging file folder holder and spray-painted it gold and converted it into a hair caddy. I mounted it to the wall and placed all of my hairbrushes, flat irons, and my blow dryer in it.

I like to use bookends to divide my purses on the shelf in my closet, so they stay upright and it's easier to pull them out without dragging all the other bags with it. Amazon and Walmart have sets of 10 or 12 for around $20-$30.

Dollar Tree shower curtain rings placed on the base of a triangular hanger are great for organizing and storing scarves.

Two- or three-tier shoe organizers over 24" in length are great for horizontally stacking and storing backpacks, duffle bags, small pocketbooks, clutches, or floppy bags with no structure.

The IKEA kallax four-cube vertical cubbies, if placed horizontally, double as a bench for kids for reading nooks and mud rooms. The eight cubes (4x2) are great for adults, check the dimensions to see which option works best for you. Above the kallax you can place some hooks on the wall or mounted coat rack and create a homemade mud room.

Cardboard boxes covered in contact paper, for decor, are excellent for storing snacks or organizing a pantry, making it easy to pull out the box and see what is in them. This idea is excellent for deep cabinets.

My friend takes soup cans, cleans them out, covers them with elegant contact paper, and uses them to store her pens. She lets the rims stick out, so they have a very shabby, chic look. She also takes the large tomato sauce cans and uses those to store some of her cooking utensils.

Turn short vases into storage containers.

Keep all your glass beverage bottles (Snapple, Kombucha, etc), take off the labels, scrub off the residue, and use them as water bottles.

Keep and wash glass containers (pickles, etc), remove the labels, scrub off the residue and use them as food storage containers instead of buying them. If you want to get fancy, get some black chalkboard stickers labels and a chalk marker at the Dollar Tree, Walmart, or Amazon and label them.

Repurpose a large piece of wood, flat plastic, flat metal, tempered glass, or marble as a tabletop by adding legs or a table base. You can find these online or of course at Amazon and Walmart. You can make side tables, a coffee table, a foyer table, a desk, kitchen, or dining room table depending on the size of the tabletop and the height of the legs. You might want to seal the wood if you choose to go that route.

Take old frames and go to a frame shop and ask them to add a mirrored glass to make your own mirror.

Take an old frame and tape cardboard, foam board or cork board to the back, then hang it up. You can use thumbtacks to post notes, photos, or necklaces.

Take an old frame and cover a piece of cardboard with chalkboard or whiteboard contact paper then tape it to the frame to make a framed chalkboard or whiteboard. You can also use chalkboard or whiteboard paint which is not the same as chalk paint. You can buy chalk, chalkboard markers, or whiteboard erasable markers to compliment the piece. I suggest buying an eraser unless you want to use a rag to wipe it down.

Frames can be easily found at garage sales. Take the current picture and glass out and use the frame.

Lay a small mirror on a table and use it as a perfume vanity stand.

Take any pins or brooches you may have and add them to denim jackets, coats, a backpack, or a hat.

Turn your jeans inside out and wear them that way. Just kidding. Just checking to see if you are still coherent or reading on auto pilot. Don't do that. Unless you want to do it, make a meme, and reference this book #brokeinthecity.

Donate any items you will not use to a local donation center so someone else can repurpose them.

Clothing

These are a few suggestions for clothing.

- Sewing closed any holes in shirts instead of throwing them out
- Using patches to cover holes or stains
- Using elaborate pins/brooches to cover up holes or stains
- Dying clothes to cover stains. You can tie-dye items, which is always fun, and this is also a great option for bed sheets and towels, especially if you have kids. Or you can dye light-colored stained items a dark color to hide the stain.
- Using a vest, sweater, blazer, cover-up, or an open sweater to cover a stain on a button down, turtleneck, blouse, t-shirt, or long-sleeved shirt.
- *Shoe clips. This will change your life ladies. Look up shoe clips on eBay. You can get Payless or inexpensive shoes or just use a current pair of shoes. Then buy a set of rhinestone or gold-plated shoe clips, and those affordable shoes miraculously look crazy expensive. You can even use clip-on earrings to do this!
- Take an old t-shirt or sweatshirt and cut out the collar and an additional inch or two on each side. Then, pull the shirt to one side so one shoulder is covered, and the other shoulder is exposed, creating a fashionable *Flashdance* sweatshirt look. *Flashdance* is a movie that came out in 1983 featuring Jennifer Beals. She wore this one-sided sweatshirt that looked so cool.

FOOD

Take fruits and vegetables that are about to spoil and put them in the freezer. If you decide to make a smoothie, you add the frozen fruits and vegetables instead of ice.

Freeze anything you will not eat in 24-hours and reheat later. Peeling and cutting vegetables then freezing make it easy to throw in a crock pot or the oven, especially root vegetables like onions, carrots, beets, and more. Cutting potatoes into french fries, wedges, or grating into hash browns and seasoning makes it easier to cook a quick meal. Cutting plantains when they are green and freezing them are a great way to fry plantain chips when in a rush or cut them into chunks to boil to make mangu. This will preserve the freshness and keep them from ripening. I also slice yellow ripe plantains and freeze them. When you are ready, slightly defrost them in the fridge or on the counter and fry or bake them to make Maduro. This is great for when certain items are not always available in your neighborhood supermarkets, or they are more expensive than in other areas where these are staple items. Buying them in bulk and cutting and prepping them to freeze makes them available when a craving arises and saves you money.

The green stalks that grow out of onions are chives, and they are just as delicious as the onion. Keep the onion until the chives are ready.

You can use spoiling food as compost for your plants or garden.

DIY - DO IT YOURSELF

Proceed at your own risk.

PHONES

Instead of throwing out your old 3G or older smartphones, which eventually might end up in a landfill, repurpose them as iPod touches or Wi-Fi audio listening devices. For example, an iPod touch, as of 2022, that is 16 GB, is over $100. Whereas the 32 or 64gb iPhone 5 can easily be purchased on walmart.com or anywhere for $40+. You can store music, Facetime, play games, and surf the Internet. Having a separate device for music frees up space on your phone.

They could work as a travel phone if you don't want to risk losing or damaging it on a trip. It's also a great back up phone to have around if you do lose or damage your current phone.

They are also great for kids as a toy or to prepare them for a more expensive smartphone. Donating your old iPhones to senior centers or day cares is another way to keep the constituents entertained and allows them to use it as a learning tool. I gave my father my old iPhone so we could FaceTime. Since he had a stroke and aphasia, he can't speak. This was a great way for us to see each other and better communicate without going out and having to buy a more expensive phone. Someone stole it though. I should have filed a police report but didn't think of it.

You should always file a police report if the phone goes missing. You can have it deactivated so no one could use it. In order to block the IMEI number, you will need to **register an**

FIR in a police station about your stolen/lost device. The police station will provide you with a copy of the FIR. Take the copy of the FIR to your service provider and show them the copy of the FIR. If you have an android and want an iPhone just for the facetime feature or apps that are only on iOS, an older phone might be a cost-effective solution.

3G phones are now obsolete in America, whereas earlier 4G phones should still be good for about a decade. There may be some apps that won't work unless you upgrade it, but from what I have read the iPhone 5 and older do not support upgrades past ios 10. There is an app called textPlus that lets you message on WIFI devices, but I am not sure if it works on the iPhone 5. However, it should work on newer models.

Repainting Furniture

If you get really good, you can make a business out of that and then charge people. Acquiring secondhand pieces and repainting them gives them a new life. I prefer wood over particle board because you can change the look multiple times. After acquiring a beautiful piece, Kilz primer is very effective as a first coat. Make sure the primer you use is the same base as the paint you're using. If you're using latex paint, get latex primer. If you're using water-based paint, get a water-based primer. After it dries, follow up with two to three coats of your preferred color, letting each coat dry before applying the next coat. After 24 hours, seal it or let it cure for 30 days, which means you cannot touch it. =0/ I recommend sealing it. Look up which sealants work with your paint.

I prefer to paint everything white, but you can use any color you would like. If it's an amazing piece of furniture that deserves excellent treatment and you have the patience to sand it down (with sandpaper or a sanding machine), then staining it would be an excellent option.

It's very easy to create a cohesive look to an apartment by changing a piece's color.

Faux flower bouquets

Floral bouquets brighten every room. Just go to the Dollar Tree, Michaels, Hobby Lobby, your local garden center or wherever you can find faux flowers and create beautiful bouquets by just arranging the flowers in a vase. You may want to pick up floral tape to wrap the base of the bouquets if you choose to create bouquets to lay flat on a surface. Make sure to cut the stems evenly before wrapping in floral tape if you are not putting them in a vase.

Look up instructions / recipes online for the following:

You can make your own:

Body butter or body oil with shea / mango / cocoa butters, carrier oils and essential oils
Flaxseed hair gel
Hair masks
Hair treatments
Laundry detergent
Kombucha
Beer
Pickles
Bread
Green Juice
Smoothies
Ice cream (sorbet is easier)
Sparkling water with sodastream or similar products
High-end decor - Youtube has a ton of these videos

Diy.org has great projects for kids.

Thespruce.com is great for DIY ideas. You could easily spend hours reading the suggestions there.

CHAPTER

Seven

FINDING DISCOUNTED /WHOLESALE ITEMS

Of course, you can go to a thrift shop and find discounted items but not everyone wants secondhand items. This section focuses on finding brand new items with deep discounts. Let's get started.

BUY IN BULK

I save so much money buying things in bulk or lots on eBay instead of buying it individually at a store. For the price of two deodorant sticks, I can buy 8-12 sticks. For the price of one full-price mascara I can get eight travel-size products (so they don't dry out). Even buying toilet paper and household products are cheaper per piece when purchased in bulk.

I recently discovered commercial paper towels like the ones in public bathrooms. One roll lasts me 3-4 months. I used to go through one roll of regular paper towels every 1-2 weeks. I'm single but have two roommates. They work just as well as the fluffy paper towel options, but the only thing is you have to rip it every time you use it, which doesn't bother me at all. That's probably why I am saving so much because I am only using what I need. I buy a pack of 12 commercial towel rolls on Amazon for like $20-30 and give some to my parents, and they last forever.

When you buy in bulk you end up with so many extra items that you can create great gift baskets for friends and family throughout the year for holidays, birthdays, Mother and Father's day, etc.

Buying Clothes Off-Season

This is the practice of buying things after the season. Many people I have met do this. Companies usually sell seasonal items for half off or more at the end of the season to make room for the upcoming seasonal items.

I buy all my tanks, t-shirts, lightweight long-sleeved t-shirts, maxi skirts, flip flops, and summer dresses in September when they are on sale. I buy Tory Burch flip flops in December when they are 30-50% off. I buy my winter boots, Uggs, suede fur-lined boots, winter gear, etc., in March & April when stores are preparing for spring and summer. If you are in the southern hemisphere reading this book, reverse the seasons.

I buy all my Christmas decorations and cards for the next year on the day after Christmas when everything is half off. You can have an after-Christmas friends party and get all your decorations for pennies on the dollar. I buy all my Christmas presents in June-September for friends and family, so when the Christmas sale gift sets and bundles pop up, I can shop for myself guilt-free. Also, the after Christmas sales are great to buy upcoming birthday gifts for the first half of the year.

You can buy Mother's Day gifts after Christmas or Valentine's Day when gift sets are affordable. Mother's/ Father's Day sales are great to buy items for friends who have birthdays in the second half of the year. Some of the best prices on gift sets are only available during this time. You can buy all your 4th of July BBQ items after the Memorial Day sale.

Competition Price Match

Some stores will match or try to beat a competitor's price. Look up the store you're going to and see if they have a price match guarantee. Afterward, check out some competitors that have better prices. If you know that it's cheaper somewhere else, you can buy the items that you need at a much lower price at your local store. If a store you go to doesn't match prices, at least you found it cheaper somewhere else and have the option of buying it and saving money.

Couponing

If you buy the newspaper, you can cut out coupons and use them. There are coupons for supermarkets, restaurants, local services, etc. Nowadays, you can print them online. You can just type in your search engine "**printable coupons,**" and pages pop up, usually asking you for your ZIP Code. They then provide a variety of coupons you can use in that area. Be wary of the free sample promos; some are clickbait or scams to get your info. Very few of them work or send you free samples.

There are also coupon and promo codes that you can use on almost every website. If you just type the name of the website and then the words promo code, many websites pop-up that share promo codes you can use at checkout and save money. (ex. **Bloomingdales.com promo code**) I like to use retailmenot.com

---

Beauty

Please be careful with buying knockoffs and very cheap makeup from overseas as they may not have been tested and may contain lead, arsenic, or carcinogens. Lead may affect your neurological functions. Please do your own research.. It's best to buy a quality product that has been tested when dealing with your skin.

Annual Sales

Know your annual sales! The Bath and Body Works June & December Sales are epic; I always stock up for the year at this time. Victoria's Secret's annual sale is a great time to stock up on bras and underwear. Many stores have an annual blowout sale--keep that in your calendar and budget so you have money to spend if it's a brand you spend a lot of money on.

QVC sells the Wen Gallons in June, and you should stock up June 1st because they sell out of certain scents quickly. In December are the Wen Seasonal Gift Sets (I only use the seasonal scents as the original line is too strong and makes my hair fall out.). There are great holiday gift sales from June-December so you can shop early. Christmas in July is another great time to shop on QVC. I like QVC because you can break up most payments into installments depending on the promotion. So, if you start shopping in June, you're done paying everything off in December. So, you can buy what you want for yourself during the Christmas sale season.

I only buy things on sale, and it must be an exceptional item like a Chanel bag for me to consider paying full price. Those are investment pieces though, and they are classic prestige bags. Plus, they have a great resale value.

Beauty Counters

This one is iffy. If you have a special occasion, you can put on a whole face of makeup (quickly) for free at a beauty counter by using the samples that are out. I would not do this myself, but I know people that have. Keep in mind there may be bacteria on them. Wipe down and spray alcohol on the lipsticks; never use gloss because some people use the wand and put it right back in. Ugh. Now you can't do this every day on a consistent basis but if you have a place where they have different counters, you can do it once a week at a different counter, and if you're in the city, they have multiple stores like Sephora, Macy's, or Nordstrom where you can just run in and do a quick makeup and leave. (Keep in mind this is not the most sanitary option because other people are using these products as well.)

When I did professional makeup, we were always told to spray the products with alcohol. You can ask them if they have a spray bottle of alcohol because you want to try something and you don't want to get other people's germs on you. You can spray the products before you use them, and that should sanitize it to a degree. Spray the brushes as well or bring your own. Don't make a habit of this not only because it's rude, but they'll catch on, and you may get in trouble. This for special occasions when you are super broke or need a quick touch-up. Sometimes if you buy something that you were going to buy anyway, they'll do your makeup for free in hopes that you buy more makeup. Oh, and when you do buy that one thing, ask for samples of everything and get as many samples as possible.

There are places like MAC where you can buy eyelashes, and they will put them on for you and do your makeup for free (not all stores follow the policy).

Beauty schools

Beauty schools are often looking for models that they can use so that the students can practice on. So, you can get free services like make up, haircuts, hair coloring touch ups etc if you volunteer at beauty schools. Sometimes these services are free or deeply discounted.

Craigslist Free

There are always beauticians giving away free haircuts, free waxing services, and free everything because they need to practice. So, keep in mind it's a student that needs to practice so don't be upset if you don't like it, but at least it's free if you have no money. Please be mindful and tip.

Dental schools

Similar services work for dental schools. If you are looking to get a cleaning or need to get a cavity filled, you can volunteer so that the students at the dental school can practice on you.

I would only go for a cleaning and x-rays. I'm very hesitant to let people practice on me for any real dental work, but if you know you have a cavity or need dental work and do not have dental insurance, you can have them practice on you. If you need anything more significant than that they may offer you those services at a large discount.

Ebay Makeup

You can get affordable pieces online or buy bulk lots of makeup. You can either buy particular brands in lots (search the brand + the word "lot," i.e. Jeffree Star Lot), or you can just type in makeup lot or makeup bulk and see what pops up. Also, my trick here is to buy travel size makeup. For the price of one full size, you can get multiple travel sizes that exceed the size of a full-size, and you're getting it for sometimes up to 80-90% off. I do this mostly for my luxury skincare. There was one moisturizer I used, which cost $129 per ounce. They sell four of the .5 ounce (2 oz total) of the travel sizes for $22, so I end up saving over $100, and I still get more of the product than if I bought the full size.

Many products last longer with travel sizes because once you open certain high-end products, you have to use them right away because they lose their potency once air hits them. With the travel sizes, you don't open it until you need it. When you do, it's such a small amount that you're able to go through the tube and still maintain the potency.

Lastly, when purchasing anything online, always look for the set, kit, or gift. So, if you like Chanel, look up Chanel gift, or

Chanel set or Chanel kit, and you'll get the full-size product you were looking to purchase, and as a bonus, you receive additional items for free.

Ebay Perfume

Buy tester perfumes at almost 50% off. They are the real parfum or EDT but have been labeled as a tester or sprayed a few times before someone decided to take it off the floor and sell it. Search the term tester perfume and then your favorite brand.

Parks and Recreation

A great way to get in shape or keep fit in New York is at NYC Parks and Recreation facilities (look it up). They have multiple gyms and programs throughout all five boroughs you can go to for one low price. Currently (2019), it's $75 for six months or $150 for the year, and you can use the pool in the facilities that have pools. It's free for children up to 16 years old, and I believe it's $50 for seniors for the whole year. This is a far more affordable option than most gym memberships.

Samples at Beauty Counters

Most beauty and perfume counters at malls or department stores have samples, and if you ask for them, they will give them to you. If you make it a habit and don't buy anything, they'll stop giving them to you. I suggest buying something periodically to keep getting those samples. When you make a purchase, always ask for samples.

Walmart

I was astonished when I found out the brands Walmart carries. I buy expensive perfume, and for some reason, Walmart gets them half off. They even sell Creed! That was shocking. So, I suggest getting it either on eBay or Walmart because these prices are ridiculous. They smell the same. I haven't had a bad one yet. If you do get a bad one, they'll just refund you the money they have a generous return policy. My favorites are Kenzo Amour (orange bottle only), Elie Saab Le Parfum, La

Perla Just Precious, YSL Libre intense, Hanae Mori Butterfly, Christian Dior Pure Poison, Lolita Lempicka, and Oscar De La Renta EDT.

Wigs

If you can't afford to go to the salon or you are having a terrible hair day, wigs can be your best friend! You can buy really affordable wigs on eBay, Amazon, Walmart, wigs.com, and local beauty supply stores sometimes have wigs. I always try to get the clearance wigs. Even a ponytail or a half wig will work.

Ponytails can be used by slicking your hair back, and then you just clip the ponytail on or tie it on. You can wrap a scrunchy, headscarf, or some hair from the wig to cover the line of demarcation (where your hair meets the ponytail).

Then there are half wigs. Half wigs are just what they sound like: they are wigs that clip onto the middle or front of your head. You can section off the front part of your hair forwards and attach the wig at that line flowing toward the back of the head. Then you release the hair that was sectioned off in the front and allow it to fall on the wig and blend the two (your hair and the wig) together. Or when you are too lazy or your hair is too jacked up that day, you can slick your hair back. Clip the half wig on top of your hair and then cover it with a headscarf or hat. I like Doores Wire Hair Extension on Amazon.

Then there are full wigs that you can just use as a regular wig, or ones you can use with a headscarf, headband, bandana, trendy hat, beanie, or even a baseball cap. Many YouTube videos show you how to make a wig look better. People trim them, pluck them, dye them, style them, wash them, blow dry them, etc.

ENTERTAINMENT

We all love to be entertained. Most people go to the theater, movies, recreational centers, night clubs, bars, restaurants etc. Below are some suggestions on how I saved a lot of money on my cable bill and exposed myself to new venues and found things to do so I could get out of the house.

CABLE TV AND WIFI

I was paying $240 with Spectrum for one box, DVR service, phone (which I only chose because it was a package deal that was cheaper than the other two services), and high-speed Internet. I discovered if I just paid for the high-speed Internet, and the time Warner cable app which allowed me to stream all the Time Warner cable channels excluding the premium channels, have limited DVR (certain shows but you can't fast forward or rewind), and an option to add premium channels for an additional amount, I was ok with that. My bill went down to $130 a month because we have the fastest Internet that they provide. Anything that I couldn't watch during the season because I did not have the premium channel. I waited for to appear on Netflix.

Since writing this section, I eliminated the app and only have the fastest WIFI. I have a Roku, and I catch up on my shows on the CW or Netflix when they come out. My bill dropped to about $70. I'm pretty sure prices are much more affordable outside of New York.

EVENTBRITE, GOLDSTAR AND UNIVERSE

Eventbrite.com promotes several events, expos, experiences, networking events, one-on-one personal classes, group classes, and more that are free and others that require the purchase of a ticket. You can promote your own events or classes there as well. I promote many of my events on

Eventbrite. If you are an entrepreneur, it is a great platform to sell tickets for your event.

Goldstar.com is great for events and shows. They have super low prices and sometimes comped events (with a service fee) to shows, concerts, plays, events, action parks, and activities. You can visit **www.goldstar.com** and see what is available near you. I love their dinner theater promotions, live jazz events, and drag brunch promos. Goldstar promotes more theater-based events than the other two.

Universe.com is another platform like Eventbrite. Several events are promoted on this platform, and you can also promote your event on the site as well.

MEETUP

This is an excellent place to meet people. Many of my clients that move around often go to meetup.com to get their first interaction with people. A lot of their events are free, and some require ticket purchases. This is a great platform for meeting people and engaging in more social events and activities. Another great place for entrepreneurs to find new clients. **Meetup.com**

MOVIES

Option 1: Movie tickets

My present-self thanks my past-self for buying discount movie tickets in bulk. This is a sure-fire way to beat inflation. So, in 2009 I purchased like 20 to 30 movie tickets for $6.75 from **Travelzoo.com** or_**Workingadvantage.com**

I recently used the last one. I've looked to buy more tickets and now they are $8.75-$10 which is still a significant savings from buying a ticket at the theater $14-$18 forget Imax or 3D prices; they are insane. I remember when it used to cost $3.50 to watch a movie.

Recently they started offering eTicket versions. I prefer the hard ticket because I may delete the email by mistake and lose all the codes.

I suggest buying them in bulk, meaning buying like 5 to 20+ tickets because as the prices go up, you're saving money while combating inflation.

Option 2: Movie Pass (the app) or AMC Movie Pass

Now, this service may not exist after this book is written as many companies are offering their version of this. AMC currently offers $20 for three movies a month. However, they got this idea from the original movie pass.

MoviePass is an app, and they send you a debit card that allows you to pay and view three movies a month for a flat rate of $15 a month. The terms may change as the company evolves. It's a subscription, so it renews every month whether you use it or not. It is limited to individual theaters and certain showings (movies) per day, but I'm not very picky, so that works for me.

Now, if I have friends who want to see a particular movie at a specific theater, that's when the bulk tickets that I purchased come in handy.

Groupon.com /Pulsd.com /Travelzoo.com

If you are familiar with Groupon, then get excited to learn about Travelzoo.com and Pulsd.com. These are sites that allow you to purchase activities and promotions at a fraction of the price. You can get up to 25+-80+% off of concert tickets, movie tickets, event tickets, excursions, travel, dining, products, experiences, activities and more.

All of the sites promote packages you can purchase, but please note you can rarely, if ever, get a refund. If you don't use it, you can use the certificate's face value as a credit at the participating location on the certificate. If and only if the venue has closed or will not honor the certificate's face value may you possibly receive a refund or credit to apply toward another purchase. The deals on these sites are so crazy good that paying full price is futile once you see how much you can save you will rarely pay full price again.

I remember my sister mentioned wanting to see Billy Joel and I found tickets on Travelzoo for 50% off!

Groupon has a wider geographical reach than Travelzoo, and Pulsd is mainly in NY as of 2021. All the sites have restaurant deals that generally offer 2 for 1 prix fixe meals, where two people dine for one price. Sometimes they offer discounted meals or discounts on your bill. My favorite website for Michelin rated meals is Travelzoo, and Pulsd has some occasionally.

Since I am in NYC, I use Pulsd more often. This website also lists a lot of free events and free tastings. They have dinner promotions for $29+ for two people to enjoy a total of two entrees and a bottle of wine; sometimes, they cost more depending on the restaurant. The higher priced promotions included more courses per person and may or may not include alcohol. They promote boat rides, networking events, food tastings, beer fests, etc., and many times the deals are "2 for 1," or you will get a significant discount on a single ticket. I sometimes buy these promotions for myself, and I go alone and meet new people. It's a great way to network and meet like-minded individuals. Actual pricing per event and certificate varies; I'm just giving examples.

You still have to pay tax and tip after the meal, and they do add that to the end of the bill most of the time. Always check for gratuity; sometimes they don't add it, so please be kind and tip.

Sometimes you have to make a reservation, and sometimes you don't, it just depends on the deal, but it's how I survive and have fun in New York. I go out and socialize at least one to three times a week because of all the things you see in this book. I also use these to take friends and family to dinner for their birthdays or special occasions. So, I look like I'm covering an expensive meal; meanwhile, it's just a promotion. I was living like a queen on the budget of a pauper.

Groupon and Travelzoo have various travel deals, from weekend getaways to weeklong vacations. Some even include flights.

My favorite deal ever was on Travelzoo in 2019 for Ai Fiori, a 3-star Michelin rated restaurant where they had a seven-course meal with wine pairing for $350 per couple. It's typically $320 per person with the wine pairing (which includes a glass of wine with each course which equates to seven glasses of wine per person!). So, getting it two for one was astonishing. I bought two promotions right away and treated my colleagues and a friend out to a fine dining experience that I still cherish. I ended up paying $700 for the promotion plus $300 in tax and tip. $1000 for a dinner for four may seem like a lot but it's about the experience. It's more expensive now but still a good deal.

Every year a select group of friends and I treat ourselves to extraordinary (ordinary for me) 5-star rated dinners ranging from $150-$500 per person, usually including a wine pairing. So, when I find a deal like that, we all get excited. Travelzoo has a lot of Michelin rated restaurant promotions. In my opinion, Travelzoo has more high-end promotions.

Subscription Television Services - Hulu/ Netflix / Disney + / HBO Max etc.

Many people have given up their cable packages for streaming services.

Disney+ is great for families or adults whose inner child is wide awake.

Hulu is great for people who have TV shows that they want to watch and only have WIFI (no cable service). Hulu has various shows you can watch the day after they air. It's far more affordable than cable especially if you combine it with Netflix. When they go public, buy their stock. They will probably get acquired by another streaming service first. Then you buy that stock before the buyout.

Netflix is super cheap, but it keeps getting more expensive every year. Pretty soon, it's going to be like another cable service. Right now, it's relatively affordable. If you have a Roku, there are so many channels where you can access free movies, and you may just have to endure some commercials.

HBO Max lets you see some great options offered on HBO through a streaming platform. I believe HBO Max replaced HBO Now.

During the pandemic many people were able to pay a premium cost to watch movies that would normally be released in theaters on Disney+ and HBO Max in the convenience of their homes. That is how I was introduced to these services.

$1 PIZZA SLICE

There are so many dollar pizza slice places all over the city. Just look it up. It's usually one dollar for a cheese slice, and it costs more if you want a topping.

123 BURGER SHOT BEER

Right now, it's located at 738 10TH AVE., Manhattan West Side3, NY, NY, 10019 212-315-012 and Harlem 712 W 125th St NY, NY 10002. They serve $1 burger sliders, $2 shots, and $3 beers (domestic on tap) all the time along with an American Sports Bar themed menu selection.

APPS

Avoid using any food delivery apps with a delivery fee and service charge. Sometimes you order one thing and end up paying a delivery charge plus a service fee and then a tip, which could add $3 to $10+ to your order. Basically, the delivery company wants to charge you so they can pay the driver, and they also want to make sure they make money, so they have a service fee. I do suggest you always tip. It may not seem like a lot, but when you add it up multiple times a week times multiple weeks per year, you could spend a couple hundred dollars or more on these fees. I suggest trying to call the restaurant directly and see if they have delivery, then you won't have to pay the service fee or delivery charge. Sometimes, the prices they give you when you call are lower than advertised online. Therefore, you save even more by calling in.

COOKING AT HOME

The best way to save money is to cook at home. You can cook on a Sunday and prepare meals for the entire week if you don't mind eating the same thing over and over. You can make a base of rice, quinoa, pasta, or steamed vegetables and then add a protein. Place them in storage containers (you can buy them at the Dollar Tree or Walmart always has good deals on storage container sets) that can go in the freezer and freeze them. You can reheat them throughout the week. Most frozen meals last anywhere from two to three weeks or longer, so you don't have to eat everything that week. You could skip some meals and eat them the week after. My friend loves to make chili then freeze and reheat it. I am Dominican, so I love to make sancocho!

Always take food with you and pack snacks for work if you're on the go when you get hungry. I like to buy a big bag of pretzels from the Dollar Tree and then a bunch of nuts from **nuts.com** or the Dollar Tree and then create a trail mix that I take with me in little baggies, so when I'm hungry, I could snack on them. Sometimes I put salt, turmeric, cayenne pepper, and other spices in the bag and shake it up so that it's seasoned.

I'm a 15-minute cook, so all of my recipes are 15 minutes or less, including prep time. I might write a cookbook about that in the future. I use a pressure cooker and a slow cooker a lot because I like food that tastes like a home-cooked meal, but I don't have the patience to sit there and cook in the oven or on the stovetop if it's more than 15 minutes. There are so many more things I want to do with my life than spend a day or a few hours cooking. It's not my thing. There are people out there who love to do it, so I would let them do that, and I will do the entertaining.

Discounts before closing

Sometimes bakeries and other businesses that create fresh products daily offer discounted items one hour before closing. They would rather sell it at a discount than incur a full loss and throw them out.

Doggy Bags

When I grew up, taking the leftovers after a meal at a restaurant was called doggy bagging. Well, if there was food leftover, whether it was mine or my friends', and they weren't taking it home, I would. I know some people thought that was tacky, but I didn't care because I had great food the next day when I was hungry. That was more money in my pocket because I didn't have to buy food that day and as you know, I don't enjoy cooking. I can't bear to think of how much food gets thrown out. If I saw a homeless person on the street, I would usually give them the bag.

Ethnic Supermarkets

I find it more affordable to go to an ethnic area to buy food directly from that supermarket if I'm trying to save money on groceries or buy authentic ingredients for certain dishes. I've had so many great conversations with people in the supermarket who gave me recipes and suggested certain ingredients to create a new dish.

Happy Hours

Drinks are always more affordable at happy hour. You can sometimes find specials on appetizers and certain dishes. So, if you're on a budget and you want $.50 wings, or sometimes $.25 wings, look for a great happy hour.

Happy hours come and go, but the ones that I'm about to mention are tried and true. These have been going on for as long as I can remember. Since the pandemic, many of the original locations listed below have closed. I have listed the ones that are still open as of March 2022.

One of my favorite places to go to since college is **Wicked Willy's**. It has changed names several times over the years, it's currently Wicked Willy's, but it's always the same location with great music and $2 dollar beers on Monday nights. Check to see if this is what the specials are, as they do change frequently. Wicked Willy's 149 Bleecker St, New York, NY 10012 Tel 212-254-8592 https://www.wickedwillys.com.

Off The Wagon has $1 mugs of domestic beer and $10 pitchers of domestic beer on tap on Monday. They have $10 pitchers of domestic beer on other days, but you have to check out the website. They are located at
109 MacDougal St New York, NY 10014 212-533-4487 www.offthewagonnyc.com.

Another honorable mention are **speakeasies.** Yes, they still exist. They're all over New York City, just look up Speakeasy NYC and see what pops up. I just had to mention it because if you're coming to New York or living here, you might as well go and check that out. They're not cheap, but they're so much fun, and they're exciting.

You can look up happy hours in your area and see what deals are available. Key phrases you might want to look up are $1 beers, 25 cent wings, 50 cent wings, happy hour, or any other term you may be interested in. Happy hours do tend to change, so it's a good idea to check periodically. However, the ones that I mentioned above have been consistent for about a decade.

Lunch Specials

When I was low on cash and did not want to cook, I would order two or three of the Chinese food lunch specials, which were about $3-4 dollars cheaper than a combination plate that was available at night. That way if I was hungry in the evening, I could just reheat it. I did that with any restaurant that had a lunch special. If the price was significantly lower at lunch.

Potluck Dinners

This is when you host a dinner or you are invited to a dinner, and everybody is supposed to bring a dish. To prepare for this, you go to the Dollar Tree and get paper plates, cups, utensils, maybe a pitcher unless you have enough plates and cups for everyone at home and you're OK with doing the dishes.

If you're hosting it, you tend to be the person that provides the animal protein unless you're a vegan, and this is a vegan potluck. If you are hosting, the benefit of this is that everybody usually takes a plate of food home (everyone should bring their own storage containers) and whatever's leftover you get to keep! The leftovers should keep you going for a few days. Whatever you can't eat, freeze and reheat later unless it's a salad.

You have to let everybody know how many people are coming so they know how much food to make. People should make a large amount so everyone can eat a decent portion.

If you're really on a budget, you could say you're making the rice (my friend Lila makes the best coconut rice), pasta, or mashed potatoes (all you need to get is a BIG box of instant mashed potatoes and milk, butter and at your discretion roasted garlic or Parmesan cheese). You can pick up a packet of peas and carrots. Add that to the rice or mashed potatoes. If you buy these items at the Dollar Tree, it should cost less than $6 for everything.

Always check for food allergies when you have a potluck. You want to make sure that everyone can enjoy the food.

I have an annual potluck dinner every year to unite my friends and family for one day, so at least I could see them once a year because everyone is so busy. It's always amazing. I order food from a restaurant and pay $50 or less for a tray of food because I don't cook. FYI if you are a guy that's falling in love with me, remember I'm not a cooker. You can't change me.

If you are not good at cooking, you can pick up pre-made salads from the supermarket, or you can go to the Dollar Tree and get about three to five packs of the frozen ravioli and a can of tomato sauce. Boil the pasta and either pour the sauce on top of it or keep it on the side to add it later. At my last dinner, I bought the best Chicken Francaise from the deli. I purchased seven pieces and had them cut them in half, so there were more pieces in case anyone wanted seconds. Always ask for extra sauce.

If you're really on a budget, say you'll bring up the bread and bring like two loaves of Italian bread. All of these are also great suggestions on how to feed yourself or your family on a budget.

Prix Fixe

I always look up Prix Fixe Meals / Lunch / Dinner. These are meals that usually come with a special menu that includes two to four courses from a select menu. It's a flat rate, and it's generally very affordable. There are many places in the city where you can find insanely affordable prix fixe lunches, like $12 for three or four courses. They can go from $9-$30+ for lunch and then from $20-$60+ for dinner.

Restaurant.com

This option saved me from staying home of boredom. I was able to socialize with friends and still cover half the bill when I was low on cash.

I purchased a bunch a **Restaurant.com** certificates when they had their annual Mother's Day / Father's Day sale, and I held on to these things for like five years (they do not expire). When I needed them and was super broke and wanted to go out with my girlfriends, I pulled out my **restaurant.com** certificate and offered to pay half the bill if they covered the rest of it, plus the tax and tip; everyone was happy about that.

This is how it works. You buy a **restaurant.com** certificate for denominations of either $5, $10 (usually cost $4), $25 (usually cost $5), $50 (usually cost $10), or $100(usually cost $20). The cost varies depending on what sale you purchased it from. You can buy blank certificates that can be used at any **restaurant.com** location, or you can buy the certificate for a specific restaurant. You can always exchange a certificate for a blank certificate later, if you change your mind or the business closes.

The denominations could be used for most restaurants if you spend twice as much as the value of your certificate. You must dine-in. They cannot be used for take-out. For some restaurants they require you to spend three times as much or more. Look at the terms before buying a restaurant certificate to see how much you need to spend to redeem it.

For example, if I'm using the $25 certificate, I would have to spend more than $50, and in some instances more than $75, depending on the restaurant. If I wanted to use the hundred-dollar certificate, I would have to spend $200. You have to look at the fine print for each location because each restaurant has different requirements. I only chose restaurants where I had to spend twice the amount, not three times.

I would tell my girlfriends, "I have a $100 gift certificate to this restaurant. We have to spend $200. I'll cover the first $100." Most people were excited because we could get more food and beverages. Call beforehand to confirm you can use the certificate for alcoholic beverages. These are great for wine bars that may let you use it on alcohol. My meals were always covered, and my friends were still spending less because when you divide the difference between the remainder of the bill and the number of people, it's less than what we would've paid if we just split the full amount of the check. It's a win-win for everyone.

If you're really struggling, everyone can pay their full share of the bill. When people put cash in the middle, you can take money back and get paid to eat. It's as if you're putting $100 in (or whatever denomination you chose), you're covering your share, and you can get cash back or have people Venmo, PayPal, or Zelle you the difference.

The only time that doesn't work is when someone doesn't want to go to a restaurant on the **restaurant.com** site.

I would use lower denominations when I went out with fewer people. If it was just a friend and me, I might use the $25 or the $50 certificate.

Please note: Sometimes, they automatically add the gratuity and tax with the certificate. Make sure you're checking the receipt because if the gratuity is added, you don't have to pay extra for that.

It also helped me cover any friends that were going through financial difficulties. If a few of us were going out to eat, and I knew one of my friends didn't have money to spend, I would make sure the hundred dollars covered our bill, including the tip. Any remaining funds would go towards a bill for everyone else.

This is extremely useful when you have a very large family. You can purchase the $100 gift certificates for 20 bucks and save $80 on the meal. On the website, I suggest going into the "specials" section, where you can usually get bulk deals at a discount.

STREET PRODUCE

More often than not, the produce that people sell on the street is more affordable than what you will pay at the supermarket. This is a great way to snack on fruit, pick up groceries on the way home and eat an affordable lunch if you're okay with fruit and veggies. Make sure to wash them well.

SHOPPING

AMAZON PRIME

Amazon Prime is a membership service you pay annually to have packages delivered for free throughout the year. The membership fee may seem like a large upfront price to pay, but when you factor in how much you will pay for each item to ship, it makes sense. Many items arrive within one to two days. If you separate the orders and put all the same day shipping orders together, you can get those on the same day. Plus, you have access to movies, music, and e-books.

Amazon Fresh is currently included with your prime membership. This service allows you to order groceries and have them delivered to your home or business, saving you time. Some of the prices are competitive. For anything ethnic, I suggest going to Spanish, Asian, African, or Indian neighborhoods to buy as the prices are more affordable and the products are more authentic. There is usually a more comprehensive array of ethnic products in stores than online.

Black Friday / Cyber Monday Sales

When people think of Black Friday sales, they usually think of Christmas shopping or getting something big for the house. When I think of Black Friday sales, I'm thinking, what can I get for myself that will last me all year and benefit me. You can get everything you want to use throughout the year at a discount, including services.

Lyft, Via, Uber all have pre-paid bonuses for their services on these days. For example, you might spend $20, but you'll get $25 or $30 in credit (promotions vary per year and per company). This is a great way to stock up for the year on services you know you will use while earning additional free credit. This goes for many services where you can purchase credit in advance: Starbucks, food establishments, and various e-commerce sites.

I have vendors I trust. They sell essential oils, candles, sneakers, handbags, handcrafted and artisanal items, and they have great Black Friday sales. I buy whatever I need for the year on that day because I know I'm going to get a significant percentage off. Sometimes, I'll save anywhere from $1000-$4000+ to just shop on Black Friday or Cyber Monday for the things that I will need for the whole year. Especially gift certificates to utilize savings for the next year.

If there's a specific program or course you ever wanted to take, it's usually cheaper on Black Friday or Cyber Monday, so wait until then so you can take the course at up to 50%+ off.

Subscriptions are cheaper on Black Friday or Cyber Monday, so if you need to renew your Norton antivirus or MacAfee, Grammarly, Intuit, QuickBooks, and more, wait until then.

I suggest looking at your purchases over the next few weeks and write down what online services / apps you purchase from. Those arc the places that you want to save to utilize the upcoming Black Friday sales. I like to buy a lot of Fiji Water on Black Friday to capitalize on the 25-30% off.

I tend to finalize my Christmas shopping by October or November to utilize Black Friday and Christmas sales for myself.

Please be aware there are better sales than the Black Friday / Cyber Monday sales. You have to get accustomed to which sales are better for which products. After following everything in this book for a year or two, you're going to know which sales are better for what items.

Closeout Sales

With the takeover of online stores, many major brands are going out of business. This is an excellent opportunity to buy expensive stuff at a fraction of the price. Recently Lord & Taylor closed their flagship store on Fifth Avenue in December 2018. Almost everything was $5.99 to $9.99 or more in the months of November and December. I bought over $4000 worth of clothes for $350. Some items were labeled $150 each. I purchased them for six dollars each! I bought Karl Lagerfeld and Badgley Mischka sneakers that were $150 each for a total of $24 for the two pairs. This doesn't happen often, but when it does, you swear that God and his angels are shining a halo of light on you. The trumpets are going off, and you feel very lucky. Everything I bought at that sale is probably going to keep me going for the next two years. I even bought

Marmont hiking pants for six dollars in anticipation of hiking after my knee heals. (Update as of 2021, all the Lord & Taylor Stores have been closed.)

If you hear of a sale like this don't be greedy, tell your friends, because the only way I found out about that sale is because my amazing friend, Stephanie, told me. My mother and I were able to go to town and knock it out. It was what I needed the most right after the car accident as I had very little money. My mom paid for half of the items as a Christmas present, since I gained so much weight while recovering from the accident and nothing fit me. This was the opportunity I had to find clothes that we're going to fit me and look good at an affordable price. I was getting tired of Old Navy, which was the only other brand I could afford.

CVS

My favorite thing to do is go to CVS when they have specials that earn extra bucks. They always have sales where if you spend a certain amount on specific goods, you'll earn extra bucks you can use for your next purchase.

Therefore, I split my order in two, and the first order is comprised of the items that, if purchased, will generate extra bucks to use for the next purchase. When I complete the first purchase, the coupons come out with the receipt; then I use them for the remaining items in my cart. I can earn and save about $15-$20 or more. It's a win-win situation.

When you sign up for a CVS card, you receive a coupon every month for 25% off a regularly priced item. Not only can you get money to use for your second purchase, but you can also get 25% off a regular priced item and use the extra bucks to pay for that item.

DOLLAR TREE

Note: Everything from here down is about the Dollar Tree until you reach the Rakuten / Top Cashback section. Dollar Tree has recently increased their prices from everything being $1 to $1.25.

The dollar store is convenient for stocking your home with cleaning products, shower curtains, bathmats, kitchen items, party supplies, cat litter pans, pet treats, stuff for your vehicle, gas treatment, etc.,

I love the Dollar Tree with everything in my soul. I still shop there and always will. They get many unique things from Michael's and other name brand locations that are getting rid of their inventory to prepare for new stock.

I love buying office & party supplies, pet toys and snacks for my cat, cleaning supplies, and organizing supplies here. When shopping for food at the Dollar Tree, I try to look for items with four ingredients or less in all categories. However I will indulge in Puffed Cheez Doodles, Voodoo New Orleans flavor Kettle Chips, Boom Chick a Pop Popcorn, and Kettle Popcorn.

Bathroom Supplies - Soap, deodorant, shower curtains, toiletries, back scrubbers, loofah sponges, toothpaste, toilet scrubbers, mouthwash, curly hair products, travel toiletries, cleaning supplies and cleansers, soap dishes, storage containers, and so much more.

Car and Home Improvement supplies - Air fresheners, gas treatment, tire shine spray, screwdrivers, duct / electrical tape, lightbulbs, nails, screws, tape measure, antifreeze, brake fluid, transmission fluid, and so much more.

Food - Now, each store is different, and the items they carry vary depending on the demand. They have eggs, milk, butter, large bags of French fries, frozen vegetables, frozen ravioli, canned foods, nuts, dips, salsa's, pasta, full-size bags of name brand chips, and snacks great for Halloween, soda, and more.

Bottled water (A gallon or six - 16.9 ounce bottles of water can be purchased for $1.25 + tax total in my area). I can't speak for the country. This is perfect for camping, handing out bottles to homeless people, everyday use, events, and parties.)

Gardening Supplies and Faux Flowers - You can buy plastic pots and sometimes ceramic pots, seeds, gardening tools, fake / faux flowers for bouquets, vases, pebbles, and rocks / fillers for the vases, bouquet tape, etc. Sometimes the bouquets you can make with faux look better than real flowers.

Household Supplies - Brooms, generic Swiffer refills, microfiber cloths, bleach, buckets, mops, laundry supplies, and cleaners

Kitchen - glassware, utensils, plates, pitchers, storage containers, strainers, dishwashing liquid / tablets / powder, oven mitts, dish rags, placemats, Lysol wipes, etc. Some of my chic clients buy their plates and cups at the dollar store. I was shocked, too.

Office / School Supplies - Stationery, pens, thank you notes, holiday cards, pencils, marble notebooks, small to large notebooks, and other supplies

Party / Event Supplies - If you're having a party, going away for the weekend, or camping, they have many disposable items at very affordable prices. They have great decorations, gift bags, a variety of notecards, cups, paper plates, hamburger / hot dog buns, bread, condiments, pickles, Halloween candy bags, Halloween candy, everyday candy, graham crackers and chocolate for S'mores, soda, snacks, excellent cards for a variety of events and themes so you can stock up for Mother's Day, Father's Day, birthdays, and holidays.

Just go there, and you'll see. Again, each Dollar Tree is unique and carries a mixture of different items. The Dollar Tree is very different from the dollar store. You can go to **dollartree.com** and buy things in bulk however, you usually have to buy three to twenty-four of each specific item. Each item has a minimum quantity you need to purchase for delivery. If you have a large family, you can always stock up.

DOLLAR GENERAL

Sometimes Dollar General has better deals than the Dollar Tree because of the $0.25 pricing increase at the Dollar Tree. There are a lot of items at Dollar General that are still a dollar that are now $1.25 at the Dollar Tree. If you have a manufacturers' coupon, you can get it for even less!

Sometimes manufacturers' coupons are stackable so you can use more than one on the same product! if you sign up for the app you will receive a five-dollar coupon every Saturday for free. It's only valid on that Saturday, it's not redeemable during the week.

If you sign up for their text messaging notification, they will send you coupons you can stack with that five dollars free weekly coupon from the app or with the manufacturers' coupons. To subscribe to DG Mobile Alerts, text SIGNUP to 34898 (DGTXT).

There's a limited number of coupons you could use per order, but you can separate your orders to utilize all the coupons. Also, if your coupon is greater than the value of the item you're buying, you get a credit for that difference to use in the same order.

On Tuesdays some items from Two to Four Seasons ago get marked down to a penny. You can find this information online on their store website. On the app you can scan the barcode, and it will show you how much the item is. If it says $0.00, it's a penny.

RAKUTEN/ TOP CASHBACK - Get Cash Back

I used to use Ebates, which is now Rakuten, every time I shop online. I have made over $900 in refunds just for doing the same shopping that I would've done anyway. I just clicked on Ebates before I made the purchase. It's ridiculous not to use it. These cashback websites are always changing their names so just search for "**cashback purchases**" online.

EBAY

Lastly, my number one go-to is eBay. For some reason, people think it's difficult, but I find it extremely easy. I like to filter the items' location to North America or the United States, so it arrives quickly. Anything from China or elsewhere can take one week to 1 month or longer. Then, I sort it by the lowest price, if I'm looking for the most affordable price.

If I want a price cheaper than that, I'll switch the filters to auction and then change it to time ending soonest. That way, whatever is ending right away within the next 1 to 5 minutes, I will bid on and usually win. If you get into a bidding war, just wait until the last fifteen seconds. Then, when you get to about 10 seconds, type in your bid and press enter. You're likely to win if someone doesn't have a higher bid in already.

My favorite items are open-boxed items on eBay. You can get Dyson's, Beats headphones, all types of electronics half-price. I recommend always buying insurance, so you don't have to worry about future issues.

eBay Bags / Wallets

You can get Chanel bags on eBay starting at $800, Gucci, Bally, Balenciaga, Bottega Veneta, Ferragamo, Louis Vuitton, YSL, and more, all at huge discounts. Now, learning how to spot real vs. fake is important. I had to watch several YouTube videos and read many articles that showed how to spot a fake. Chanel, Louis Vuitton. Fendi and Gucci were always easy for me as I've only ever had the real thing, so I could spot a fake from 10 feet away. Almost all my wallets are second hand as I can't justify spending more than $100 on a wallet. I prefer vintage blue Gucci jacquard to the new lines.

Five Below

I recently discovered this store, and it is awesome. Everything is between $1-$5. They have a lot of quality items and gadgets for great prices. You can order items online at **www.fivebelow.com**

Gift Cards

I like to buy gift cards in advance for myself with the discounts mentioned below. If I am ever low on cash or in need of emergency cash, I can always use the gift card to save the day. This helped me tremendously during the pandemic. I had so many gift cards I just lived off them. I bought Starbucks, McDonalds, Kohls, Amazon (kept the code and redeemed it when I needed it), movie passes, supermarket gift cards and more. Also, they are great for last minute gifts.

Gift card sites like raise.com, giftcardwiki.com, cardcash.com, or cardcookie.com allow you to buy discounted gift cards. So, you can get anywhere from 1% to 20% or more off a gift card price, resulting in immediate savings when you purchase something at the corresponding retailer. You can also sell any of your unused gift cards to many of the above-mentioned sites.

If any of the above websites cease to exist, you know what to do. Just search online for discounted gift cards. Make sure to do your own due diligence, and check to make sure they're not a scam website. You can do this by typing in the name of the website and the word scam. Articles will pop up mentioning if they are a scam. There are also sites that monitor scam sites like trustpilot.com and scamadvisor.com. Sometimes you must enter the .com, nyc, .gov or whichever suffix the site has for it to find the site. Sometimes you have to add the www. or https:// if you see an error code.

Lowe's

Lowe's cuts wood, electrical wiring, shelves, carpet, pipes, chains and blinds for free.

If you're doing small projects but you don't need to buy a machine because you don't use it often you can rent it at Lowe's.

There are also buying bulk sections in store and online that give you discounts when you buy multiple items. This is great for small projects or home renovations.

If you will spend more than $1500 at Lowe's go to the pro center (you do not have to be a business or contractor, you just have to spend over $1500. This only works prior to purchasing not after purchasing) and let them know what you want to buy and they may give you a volume discount. This is great if you're doing renovations.

Lowe's price matches many online retailers like Bed bath and beyond, Amazon.com, Wayfair.com, Walmart.com, Target.com, Home Depot.com, Best Buy.com, Macys.com, JCPenny.com, bedbathandbeyond.com

You can pay $19 for 90 minutes to rent a vehicle at Lowe's to drop off your stuff. It's cheaper than a U-Haul if you're going to spend less than an hour and a half dropping off the items. Pricing can change depending on location and when you read this book versus when it was published.

OLD NAVY

They recently introduced this Super Cash Promotion, similar to Kohl's cash with Old Navy, for every $25 you spend within a specific timeframe, you're going to get $10 Super Cash (which is a gift card code) to use in the future during a particular week. When that week arrives, you can redeem the $10 Super Cash code. However, there is a stipulation that you can only use $10 off of every $25 of whatever you're purchasing including sale and clearance items. If you have $40 in Super Cash, you need to spend $100 to use $40. It can be prorated, so if you only spend $50, you will get $20 off, and the remaining $20 balance is saved on that code for future use during the week or you can gift it to a friend or family member. Then the cycle repeats.

While you are utilizing the new coupons, they offer more coupons. For every $10 you get discounted for spending the $25 minimum, you get another $10 to use in a few weeks. That is how they hook you to continue buying from them every season because you don't want to lose the cash you earned. It's best to give them away if you are not using them.

I like Old Navy for staple items like T-shirts, tank tops, long-sleeve tees, vests and cardigans. Some people like their jeans, but they are not flattering on me for some reason. My waist is smaller than my booty, but if I get jeans that fit my booty, they don't fit my thighs or my waistline. So far, Ralph Lauren, Iman, Avenue (which is a plus-size store, but they have tall jeans), and Gap Curvy Boot Cut Tall jeans work for my figure. I hope that helps any curvy girls.

IKEA

Want a custom closet but cannot afford an expensive closet system? Try the pax wardrobes. Since IKEA has teamed up with task rabbit, they can ship to just about anywhere and then have a task rabbit come and assemble it for you. You're going to have to pay the shipping charge and the assembly charge, but it's still cheaper than getting a custom closet. Many of my very wealthy clients will buy IKEA closet systems without the doors and have them built in a small room or nook and make it a walk-in closet. They have another professional purchase and install crown molding on the top and bottom. You can customize them however you like. If you're handy, you can build it yourself. Good luck!

As for any other furniture, I highly recommend the Billy bookcases; if you get a bunch of them and line them up next to each other, it looks like a library. They are great for storing shoes size 10 for women / 8 for men or smaller. They are 11" in depth.

If your feet are between 16" to 11", you will benefit from the Brimnes line. If your feet are 23" to 16", you would benefit from the Pax. Clients also like to add crown molding to these, and some go as far as to adding it to the middle to cover the connecting sides that show they are two separate units.

Many people like the Besta if you want wall-mounted storage. The doors always sag after some time, and you have to adjust or replace them.

My favorite drawer system is the Hemnes. I prefer to change the knobs to give it a more expensive unique look.

They have various other items like lighting, kitchen items, linens, curtains, shelving systems, tables, chairs, indoor and outdoor furniture, beds, etc.

If you would like to get a discount, they have the IKEA family card that is free to register for and get additional discounts during sales. I should be getting paid for all this advertisement.

Male Gifts

I buy male holiday or birthday gifts at Christmas time or Father's Day weekend (Clothes, Cologne Sets, Electronic Gadgets, etc.) as they usually have great gift sets that are more affordable. I have no problem shopping for these items in June and saving them to gift throughout the year. It is not advisable to buy very expensive cologne (over $100) like Creed as it may get rancid if you shelf it for too long.

Pick Up Option

Some stores like Home Depot provide a discount online but not in store. As you know, I mount TVs, shelves, artwork, and assemble IKEA furniture, so I'm continually buying tools and replacing inventory. Home Depot has an option where if you buy something online, you can save anywhere from $10-$30 on an item as long as you pick it up in the store. Meanwhile, they offer different in-store promotions. I order online for in-store pick up to utilize both. When in store, I take advantage of the in-store promotions. I pay for my items in the store and head over to the pick-up desk to get the online order, thus saving $100's of dollars. Genius!

QVC My savior. Do you hear that… those are Angels singing. The website www.qvc.com helped me tremendously. You're able to buy stuff and pay it off, usually within two to six monthly payments depending on the promotion they're offering. I was able to get my television, my laptop, my Vitamix, anything

Dyson and a bunch of other stuff and just pay them off in 3-6 payments. Lisa Robertson was my favorite host. Miss you girl. HSN and Shop NBC have good deals as well.

Rewards / Loyalty cards

Get special discounts and freebies by joining rewards programs. Baskin Robbins gives you a free cone on your birthday. Starbucks gives you a free food or drink item. 7-eleven gives out several free food and drink items depending on how much you purchase. You can save a fair amount with rewards programs. If you don't want to carry the card, take a picture of it and create a folder for your phone. Most scanners can read the barcode on your phone. You can search for "reward programs" or "loyalty programs" online and see if any would benefit you.

Sample Sales

Almost every designer has sample sales in NYC or elsewhere, where their items are sold for 50-80%off. You can go online and type in "sample sale," and sign up for various companies that send updates on the latest sample sale.

Tools

I buy all my tools during the Father's Day Sale or Christmas Sale at Home Depot, Loews, Harbor Freight, Auto Zone, Advanced Auto, etc. I utilize the pick-up option and in-store sales and save a fair amount when possible. If you know a good chain store in southern or middle America with great deals, you can order online with delivery and save more.

Walmart, Boscovs, Marshalls, TJ Maxx, Kohls or Target

The online stores in the title always have great online sales, especially after a holiday, since they need to get rid of the holiday inventory. Many stores have low purchase minimums to get free delivery. You would be surprised at how many high-end name brand items they have and how affordable they can be. Just search for something, and you'll find it. If it's not at any of these locations, it might be on eBay or Amazon.

I prefer to go into the stores when possible, as the sales in store are better than the online prices for non-holiday items.

At TJ Maxx, I purchased five pair of high-quality name brand underwear like Nautica, Jessica Simpson, Tahari, Laura Ashley, and more for $15 or less. Now, keep in mind the prices could change as the years progress.

I purchase all my candles at TJ Maxx because I have to smell them before deciding if it's worth it. Candles that are fourteen to twenty-six ounces can cost anywhere from $8 to $15, which is really affordable considering that they sell for $30-$40 at retail. The Dollar Tree candles are cheaper per ounce, but they're not as fragrant nor do they have such a wide selection.

Warning: In the last two years at TJ Maxx, I have purchased three bras that are normally priced at $50 for a total of $20 or less if they are on sale. The underwire pops out often times before the first washing. For myself, being large chested, the traditional bras like Olga and Maidenform are made very well and last for years. The inexpensive padded bras look good for the moment but do not seem to last long.

Since I live in NYC, we don't have access to an actual Walmart store. We have to go to Long Island to the one store that's out there, so I use the website. If you have a Walmart near you, I recommend going there if you need something right away.

Travel

Traveling is my favorite thing to do in the world. It is my drug of choice and what I choose to save and spend my money on. Below are my favorite tips.

Airline Flights

Based on my experience the earlier you book, the cheaper it's going to be. Booking one-way flights can sometimes be less expensive than booking round-trip. Flying into Europe on a carrier that's offering a deal like $300 or $400 round-trip is worth it. Then you connect to your desired city as connecting flights within Europe tend to be more affordable than coming from America.

I tend to book a flight into Iceland, Norway, Spain, or Portugal, and then I'll take a connecting flight to my desired city. This works exceptionally well for places like Croatia, where most flights start at $1000. I always pay hundreds less than friends traveling to the same destination. Obviously, connecting flights are priced higher, but even when my friends book connecting flights, I have paid significantly less when I connect with a different carrier.

Never search for flights on your phone or home computer. The reason is they have tracking software that records your flight inquiry. Every time you go back, the price will increase. It will never be cheaper. Using a VPN or researching on someone else's computer, IP address, or phone, allows you to search for the best rates and then after finding the best rate you can book it later on your phone. Even if you use a private window, sometimes this can happen. I am not a technician, but I have seen this happen often.

If you see a good deal, don't wait; just book it with insurance. I always take the insurance because you never know.

If your flight is more than two hours delayed or scheduled for the next day, you might be entitled to a free flight, and you have to look at your carrier contract terms. If you complain, you might get a free flight.

Booking through third-party sites like Orbitz, Expedia, or Travelocity allows you to earn points from their search engines accruing to help you earn free hotel stays. Plus, if you enter your frequent flyer miles number, you can earn points from your airline carrier and get those miles. Lastly, as we learned before, using a credit card that earns miles completes the hat trick. Earning points from three sources for the same transaction expedites your ability to redeem them.

GROUPON.COM /PULSD.COM /TRAVELZOO.COM

As mentioned in previous chapters these are sites that allow you to purchase activities and promotions at a fraction of the price. You can get up to 25+-80+% off of excursions, travel, experiences, activities and more.

Groupon and Travelzoo have various travel deals from weekend getaways to week long vacations. They have packaged local and national vacations, and travelzoo offers international getaways, some even include flights.

As a reminder all of the sites promote packages you can purchase, please note, you can rarely, if ever, get a refund. If you don't use it, you can use the certificate's face value as a credit at the participating location on the certificate. If and only if the issuing company has closed or will not honor the certificates face value, may you possibly receive a refund or credit to apply toward another purchase. The deals on these sites are so crazy good that paying full price is futile. Once you see how much you can save you will rarely pay full price again.

REMOTE YEAR AND SIMILAR TRAVEL PROGRAMS

These programs are exceptional. They allow you to travel from one month to one year around the world.

I started an instagram account where I post my travel and food experiences at www.instagram.com/wheresmayra in case you wanted to follow me on my adventures. I review food, hotels, and my experiences. I also started filming a documentary on preserving indigenous practices and learning how to heal yourself. You are welcome to follow my progress at www.theindigenousdocumentary.com. Donations are always welcome.

CHAPTER Eight

PANDEMIC INSIGHTS

Since the pandemic, I have learned a great deal. Everything in this book can be utilized but the few items listed below are specific to pandemics or region specific crises.

BARTERING

Some websites life freecycle.org allow you to list items you are giving away and ask for items you may need. The community reaches out to help you in any way possible.

DOWNGRADING AND REDUCING

Downgrade your auto insurance if you have high coverages, if you will not be driving often.

Reducing or canceling subscription services that are unnecessary, like gym memberships, online software subscriptions or memberships, hair/ make up/ pet subscription boxes/ Amazon subscribe and save items, and more.

Call your life insurance companies to use your cash value or fab account to cover your premiums for a set amount of time.

Cancel or pausing recreational activities.

Food Pantries

These pantries can be found online and provide free food during a crisis. Some cities like New York City had free food delivery for those who registered. A weekly box of food was delivered to your door for two to six weeks at a time.

Investing

I learned investing in stocks when they drop during a crisis will generally yield profits when they go back up, if they do not go out of business. I also learned certain stocks skyrocket during a crisis. Once a crisis is established, certain stocks are worth investing in during a national disaster. During the pandemic, many online businesses, delivery companies, online payment providers, gaming, medical supply companies, Crypto trading, and companies that sold physical gold and silver had a significant increase in stock prices. I'm sure there are more, but you would have to do your own research.

Utilities

Call all of your utility companies to create payment plans or see if there are any discounts they are offering. If you ask, they may offer you one.

Selling Items

Declutter and sell stuff that can bring you extra cash.

Stocking Up

Stock up on essentials without impeding on your neighbor. It's important to stock up, but if you hadn't heard, many elderly people weren't as quick or savvy to stock up. When they went shopping, there was nothing left for them. Please be mindful when stocking up, that others will also be in need.

Seriously Struggling

The following services are for people who are in dire straits. This is for people who are genuinely struggling, who really don't have the money, and are crying inside because they don't know how they will get by. If people don't truly need these services, please don't use them. Please skip this chapter because you will be taking food and services away from the people who need them to survive. There is a limited amount of food, so when the food runs out, that's it. I wanted to add this section for those that don't know where to go or what to do.

Affordable Connectivity Program

This is a program that currently reduces your cable, broadband service, or internet connected devices bill by up to $30 per month and up to $75 if you reside on tribal lands. The amount may vary as the years go by, so make sure to check the website for any changes. It was a temporary discount during the pandemic. That was recently passed as a law for individuals on SNAP, Medicaid, SSI, WIC, Pell Grant, Veterans Pension and Survivors Benefit, received a FPHA, or free and reduced-price lunch. You can check out the official page, https://www.affordableconnectivity.gov, to see if you qualify. Once confirmed, you will get a code that you must write down and provide to your provider. Not all providers participate. You only get one $30 credit per household. I suggest you view the definition of a household on the website. Certain states offer the discount on either cable, internet, or mobile phone service. Check to see what your state offers.

Back to School Events

There are charitable events in many cities that give away backpacks and school supplies before the school year starts. Please do not attend these events if you can spend $10 or $20 at the Dollar Tree, Five Below or can go to the Staples store and get the one cent notebooks when they have their back to school special. This is for families that have noooooooooooo money. Don't take something out of the hands of someone who has nothing.

Clothes

Some churches give away free clothes. Search "**churches free clothes"** to find churches in your area that are giving away clothes. Some churches also give away food.

Food Pantries

I remember when I was unemployed for a brief period. I made too much on unemployment for food stamps but not enough to cover my basic needs and pay my bills. This is a double-edged sword. If you're on unemployment, you should automatically get food stamps and Medicaid. This part of the system is ridiculous. I had to go to food pantries and wait in line and get food.

You could look up food pantries in your city, and they should have a list somewhere online. Some food pantries always have long lines, and you have to get there one to two hours early. Others have no lines. Why, I don't know. That still dumbfounds me.

If you are on the street and are starving or thirsty, small businesses and supermarkets throw out expired items that may still be edible. I'm pretty sure you're not supposed to go through commercial garbage, but if it's a hot day, and you haven't had a meal in a few days, or there's no water in sight, and they just threw out expired Gatorade or water..

God's Love We Deliver

I know this is in NYC; I am not sure if they have spread elsewhere. There is a nonprofit organization called God's Love We Deliver - **www.glwd.org** - God's Love We Deliver cooks and home-delivers nutritious, medically tailored meals for people too sick to shop or cook for themselves. To support the health of their clients, they provide ongoing nutrition assessment, education, and counseling. God's Love is a non-sectarian organization serving people in need and their children and caregivers. All of their services are provided free to clients and full of love.

Government Programs

There are several government programs you can apply for that may help you. Food stamps, Medicaid, housing lottery (look this up), and more. There are shelters you can go to and churches that provide overnight housing if you are ever homeless. There is always a way - just get good at researching information online.

In New York and California, you can get a free college education if you stay and work in the state for a certain number of years after graduation. Suppose you leave before the agreed-upon time you have to pay it back. This is a new concept, and the terms may change.

They also have government programs that deliver food if you qualify. Many people on medicaid and medicare qualify for these programs as well as others on similar programs. Meals on Wheels, God's Love We Deliver, and Mom's Meals are a few of the popular ones.

Housing Lottery

These are government-sponsored apartments you can rent or buy for a low rate compared to other units in the building. This is based on income, and you must qualify. After qualifying, you are entered into the lottery. Even if you are selected, it does not mean there will be an apartment for you as they are taken quickly, and you may not be able to afford what is left or like the location available.

It's a lottery, so chances are slim, and many lotteries require you to reapply every year. Please research extensively, as this is a great option to ensure you can afford your rent if you live in a city with quickly rising inflation rates like NYC, Miami, LA, and Chicago.

PO Box Address for Homeless Persons to Get Their Mail

In some states if you are homeless you can go to your local post office and ask how to get a PO Box address to receive mail as a homeless person. They will direct you if your state or town provides that service. You must show your ID to collect your mail and you must check every week or they will return it.

Reduced Fare Transportation

Some states or cities provide discount cards to seniors or recipients of certain low income government programs. You can search for *low-income transportation discount* or *senior discount transportation.* You might even look up the specific program followed by the word discount, and you can see what other offers other companies may offer.

Service Provider Discounts

Some service providers offer discounts to seniors, medicaid recipients, food stamp recipients, WIC recipients, and recipients of other government funded programs. If you contact your cellular phone provider, cable company, electricity provider, or gas or oil provider and ask if you qualify for a discount because you participate in a government program, they may give you a discount.

Shelters

There are many shelters throughout the US that provide room and board for a night or a duration of time. Just type in **shelter, government shelter, or city shelter** to see what is near you.

Soup Kitchens

You could look up soup kitchens online if you're starving or have a family to feed and you don't have food to cook.

CHAPTER *Nine*

CREATING EXTRA INCOME

Everyone can benefit from extra income, especially in times of duress. I have found that being good at multiple things is useful when times get a little more difficult than expected. Below are some ways to earn extra income. These methods can be used to help fund travel excursions and last-minute expenses that pop up throughout life.

BRAID HAIR

Once you learn this, you can have people come to your house, or you can go to their home and charge them anywhere from $50-$250 to braid hair. I personally have never done this, but I know people who have.

Once you have enough saved income, then you can pay for beauty school, cosmetology licensure, online courses to build your business, market it or create online courses that you can share and monetize your experience.

Latiqua Williams at **www.LatiquaWilliams.com** is an excellent person to follow and learn from. She is a world-renowned hair restoration expert. Her services and classes are listed at https://www.exxclusiveinc.com/

Please check with your state as some states require you have a license for specific hair techniques.

Capterra Reviews

This website allows you to leave reviews on a variety of software brands. In exchange, they give you a $10 gift card for each review to various places like Amazon, eBay, etc. Leave five reviews, and 30 days later, you get $50 of credit to claim the gift card. Each review takes like two to three minutes. This is the only online review website I found that pays you.

Craigslist Free

Sometimes, if I see some cool stuff that I think I could sell, I would pick it up on Craigslist free and then re-list it on Craigslist under the sale section. Other platforms to sell on would be eBay, Offer Up, Let Go, Mercari, and Facebook sales. I would look for records and books, and I would pick them up in bulk, only if they had a large lot and then I would go to book websites that buy secondhand books and then resell them.

I would research on eBay to see which records were selling and list those as record stores never give you what they are worth. Afterward, I would bring the unsold records to record stores that buy records and see what I can get there. Lastly, whatever is left, I would sell on in-person sites (Craigslist, offer up, letgo, etc.) as a "lot", never on eBay as shipping would be ridiculous, and the possibility of damage is too great. If there were one hundred records, I would list it as "Lot of 100 records." Take the whole lot no cherry picking". I would count the lot and price it for about $.25 per record. So, $.25 x number of records = price. In this case, the lot would be $25. To be honest, I would take whatever offer I get at that point. Either way, a profit is being made on the remainder of the records.

Craigslist Gigs / Resume

You can find jobs on Craigslist.org under the gigs section, jobs section, or you can post your resume under the resume section. Make sure to remove your home address and contact info to avoid getting spammed. Employers can contact you via the Craigslist email assigned to you when you pick that option.

If you're an independent contractor, placing an advertisement on Craigslist for the services you offer may help you get new clientele. You may have to pay to list gigs, jobs, and other categories. Check for your city to confirm.

Create an Online Course

People will pay you to teach them a skill. You can create videos in so many categories across so many genres. I provide consulting services that teach you how to do this, www.mayraperdomo.com.

Design Websites

I taught myself to design websites. I watched over twenty-four hours of YouTube videos on how to build WordPress websites. If I can do it, you can do it! My mom always said that.

If you specialize in a certain type like Wix, Shopify, WordPress, Elementor, Squarespace, and more, you can create a lucrative side hustle. I have faith in you.

Insurance Sales

Primerica trains you for free and provides the classes and tools you need to pass your Insurance Licensure Exam. You must pay for your test and licensing fees (they will be reimbursed← this could change) as well as $25 for POL the month before you have take the practice tests. I suggest paying the $25 about two weeks before the test; you don't need to invest in that until then.

I like Primerica because they have the best interest of their clients at heart. They paid out the most claims after 9/11 when many companies did not honor because they said it was an act of war, which voided the payout, and lastly because there are a lot of minorities in the company. That matters to me. I like being part of diverse companies.

There are many other companies like Transamerica, Aflac, and more you can look into.

Make Up

If you are great at putting makeup on other people, you can get paid for that. You can post your services on Craigslist under gigs or Facebook and post something with before and after photographs. You may have to do some faces for free to get the photos, but people will generally pay up to $50-$250 to get their makeup done professionally especially for weddings, but you have to have expensive waterproof makeup for that. As your skills improve, you can buy better brushes and makeup. You can get affordable brushes and makeup everywhere nowadays - Sephora, eBay, Amazon, etc.

Open a Bank Account

Various banks offer promos if you open a bank account with direct deposit, equivalent to a designated amount, for a specified amount of time (usually three months, it varies depending on the bank and promotion), you can earn anywhere from $150-$600. All you have to do is check online for promos, you can type in "promo open checking account" and see what pops up.

You can open an account online, or sometimes you have to go into a branch. Keep in mind you have to keep the account open for a certain amount of time after receiving the compensation. Some banks require you to keep the account open for a year. If you close the account before that, you will have to pay back the bonus. Some banks require that you have the right promo code, so don't lose it once you have it. Once you open a bank account, they will start sending you mailers with promo codes that you can give to friends and family so they can open an account as well.

I suggest having separate accounts for different things. One account for your work income, another account for savings. If you're an independent contractor, it's nice to have another account for taxes, so you don't touch that money. I was told, if you have a business, you should have seven bank accounts to keep your money separate and make it easier for your accountant. This method also helps you understand how to view your business income and structure pricing, so all of the categories below have been considered and are covered.

1. Business Income
2. Payroll
3. Taxes
4. Expenses
5. Savings / Emergency Fund
6. Personal Income
7. Personal Savings

RESEARCHING

People get paid to research all the time. I used to research on TaskRabbit. My rate was $30-$50 per hour because I was really good. I created spreadsheets, filled them with the requested information, and then sent them to the client. I included links and pictures if necessary. I went above and beyond and generally exceeded their expectations. Only twice were two people ever unrealistic. Their perception of the amount of time any human could complete the task was unrealistic. If anybody is reading this and you need someone to research, calculate the amount of time it takes to look up the info - meaning enter the search text, pull up multiple results, look through each title and click the viable ones + the seconds it takes to click on the link, have the page load, search for the info then copy and paste to the spreadsheet. It will never be under ten seconds per entry. Even if you give us one site to search, you still have to search for the info, then copy and paste.

Focus Groups: You can be part of research focus groups. You can search the term "focus groups" + the closest major city you can commute to, and you may find research companies that pay you to come in and answer questions for their database. Money4talk.com is an excellent company.

TV Focus Groups: Some companies pay you cash or gift cards to watch TV. Some pay you to install devices to your TV to monitor what you watch so they can figure out how to market to people who watch the content you view. Others monitor your computer or smartphone activity to learn what type of products similar types of people purchase like Nielsen, TVision Insights, etc.

There are online survey companies that take up a portion of your time, and the compensation is not worth it. If it takes 30 minutes for a survey and you get $5, it's not worth it. ***Make sure to research the company you will work with to ensure it's not a scam.***

Returning Bottles

I didn't like this at all, but you gotta do what you gotta do. If you're ordering items online or buying them at the supermarket and they're charging you the five-cent deposit, exchange them and get your money back. Keep those bottles, and the next time you go to the supermarket with a bottle recycling machine, get the cash and use that money to pay for part of your next purchase. If they don't have a recycling machine, sometimes you can talk to the store manager, and they'll count the bottles and pay you cash. It's your money that they're taking; you're just getting back.

Another option is you can keep the glass bottles for storage. I buy kombucha often, instead of returning those glass bottles, I peel the label, scrub it in a bowl of water with a steel pad to get the residue off, and use them for storing food like flour, sugar, nuts, beans, rice, beverages like leftover soup, coffee, tea, juice, and water. Glass storage bottles can be expensive to purchase in a store. I now reuse them and have a set of matching bottles that look great in the cupboard. I prefer glass over stainless steel or plastic.

Sharing Economy

Find a second job on a sharing economy platform like Uber, Task Rabbit, Lyft, Moonlighting, Postmates, Dumpling, Takl, Women Can Do It Too, or Handy, to name a few. This can help with additional income. Many people have used these platforms to switch careers or keep them afloat between jobs. I have been a part/full time (20-30 hours a week) Taskrabbit since 2013 because I value the time I have acquired by freelancing. I have made many business contacts and friends by completing tasks for them on the platform. My weblink is **Tr.co/mayra.**

I like the sharing economy because I make my own hours, take off when I want, and choose to work harder and take on more jobs when I want to make more money.

There are good and bad features with this option. With any new business, venture, or concept, if you get in early, you make a lot of money because the market is small, but as a market increases and competition pops up, prices drop. When I first started on **Taskrabbit.com** I made $90 an hour for specific jobs that I only make $30 an hour for now because the market is saturated, and there is so much competition. What seems like a lucrative opportunity can change quickly. My suggestion is to make as much money as you can, save it, and get prepared for the next wave of new concepts.

START A BUSINESS

I tried to find businesses I could start with very minimal costs. I learned how to create a website, a blog, and a service-oriented business.

Anything you decide to pursue will always require some manpower, effort, and time to invest in learning or mastering a new skill. In the end, it's always worth it. You can research the term "start a business for free" and see what pops up. Never enter your social security number unless you are filing for an LLC or business credit, even then, make sure it's reputable as there are many scams online. The only company I have ever trusted to start a business online is **www.amerilawyer.com**

START A DAYCARE

Currently, in NYC only, you can search in your area to see if similar services are provided. Search **start a daycare,** and you can search for **grants** if you need it.

The Committee for Hispanic Children and Families, Inc. helps people acquire the education and licensing needed to start a daycare at home. This is an excellent opportunity for stay-at-home mothers who want to stay home with their children and earn an income. It is also an excellent opportunity for anyone who wants to start their own business.

There is a cost for training. However, you should call to see if they can help. I believe there may be a few grants, so definitely inquire about that.

This information was copied from their website and may change: A registered Family Daycare Provider cares for 3 to 6 children plus two additional school-age children in a residence. A licensed Group Family Daycare Provider cares for seven to twelve children plus four additional school-age children in a residence.

The Early Care and Education Institute (EC&EI) provides training and services to established and potential child care providers looking for professional development in the early care and education field. With Spanish-speaking and culturally competent trainers, this program is a unique professional development opportunity for Latinas throughout New York City. If you are interested in becoming a New York City childcare provider or are currently a childcare provider interested in taking our trainings, please contact us at (212) 206-1090. Their website is **http://www.chcfinc.org/become-a-provider.**

START A T-SHIRT / DROP SHIP BUSINESS

I learned how to start a T-shirt business online. There are tutorials on starting your own business and many other videos from various sources on YouTube.

WRITE A BOOK

Hey, that's what I'm doing. We all have stories, and we've all been through things. As I was struggling, I told people how I was getting by, and everyone told me I should write a book. So, I did. I have no idea how well it will do, but I did it. You have stories that people need to hear to inspire them and help them. Don't hold that in. There are so many tutorials on starting and writing your eBook. I may create one. If I do, you will find it on my webpage www.mayraperdomo.com.

YOUTUBE / VLOGGING

If you have great content or an excellent idea, you can create a YouTube channel. The more views you get, the more advertisers with products that compliment your site will pay you for running ads on your page. Some people get sponsors that send them free stuff to vlog about so their product gets exposed to your customer base. Not to mention the money you can earn based on your content. Sometimes people donate to your cause or you because they like you. You can promote a product you make if you are handy or an artist; you can direct people to affiliate sites or products you promote and more. There are so many ways you can make money vlogging.

CHAPTER
Ten

I Thought You Should Know...

This chapter is filled with random information I think everybody should know. Please be forewarned; I babble a lot, and I can't help it, so I'm just going to say whatever pops into my mind. I am not a financial advisor, and the following suggestions should not be taken as financial advice. Please conduct your own research and due diligence before making any decisions. Contact a professional before implementing anything suggested in these pages.

Amazon Reviews

There are a lot of fake Amazon reviews, so in order to see if a product is truly worth it, you want to look at the most recent reviews. Click on reviews on the upper right-hand corner or scroll down to them. Then, click on the arrow pointing to the right under the title *Customer Reviews*. There should be a tab usually under the review images labeled *Top reviews*. Click that and select *Most recent*. Now, you will see the most recent reviews. I prefer to read verified purchase reviews.

Unfortunately, there are shipments that do not meet quality control standards that slip through the shipping department. You can learn if the most recent batch had an issue. Just look at the most recent reviews and you will see if the product still has consistent positive reviews.

THE BINDER

Keeping track of bills is difficult for some people and having a room full of papers may create anxiety for others. So, the system I came up with is a binder. Buy a regular binder and a hole puncher. When your bills come in, punch a hole through them and put them in the binder right away. This will avoid them piling up. Then, get dividers to divide the categories. Here are some ideas for some tabs for the dividers - due immediately, call to negotiate, call to dispute, payment plans, goals, savings, trips, and paid. Make sure to write the date, form of payment and confirmation number on the paid bill. If it is for the government, save the confirmation number and check image or money order forever. At the end of this binder section, you will find a story on why you should do that. Create categories that are meaningful to you. If you do not know where to put a category, you can create a miscellaneous category and insert it there.

If you have a payment plan, you can write how many payments remain after each bill is paid. For example, if you have like thirty payments at $30, once you make a payment, you can say twenty-nine payments left so you have an idea of how many more payments are left. Once that is done, you can transfer that $30 that you are accustomed to paying to another debt, or to an emergency fund. For example, if you've been paying $30 for 30 months and get to the last payment, you now have an extra $30 to put towards another bill, goal, trip, savings, stocks, or bitcoin Cryptocurrency. You can also keep track of your payments and bills by creating a spreadsheet on Excel or a Google Spreadsheet. If the following seems too complicated, you can download or print premade budget sheets by searching the term "printable or downloadable blank budget sheets". They also have apps for tech-savvy enthusiasts like Mint, Pocket Guard, Quickbooks, Clarity Money, etc. I prefer to do this manually.

Manual Spreadsheet:

This is how I created my spreadsheet. If you choose to do this manually, you need to start with one column to list all of your bills. You will list the months, for example, January through December, on the top row. On the column corresponding to the month, you can start putting dollar amounts that correspond to the scheduled payment. The last line of the column with the month should have the sum feature in it, meaning it adds everything up in the column for you.

Above the month, you should put your total income for that month. This is easier to do when you get a weekly paycheck. If you're like me and you're an entrepreneur, what you can do is write down all of your debts, and what the payments should be so you get an idea of what you should be paying first. As the money comes in, you start paying them based on your plan. If you have a weekly paycheck, you can put the exact dollar amounts and play with the numbers until you can get to an amount that matches your income.

You should always have a Savings category as well as an Emergency Fund category in case something happens. Adding a *Goals or Trips* category ensures you are able to do the things you love.

In the goal category, you can write down your goals as a reminder of what you are working towards. Some examples are a car, investing, a music instrument, retirement, a home, a vacation home, a boat, an event ticket, creating an LLC/ S Corp/ Corporation/ Non-Profit, getting a domain name, or the expenses necessary for you to make your side hustle a larger business. List anything you want to spend your money on when you have extra money.

This not only keeps you focused, but it teaches your children (if you have children) to mimic you and keep their finances in order as well. It gives them a base where they can start to keep track of money. I remember working for this couple, and their toddler had a birthday recently. The dad gave the child the money and asked him what he wanted to do with it. The child said, "Put it in the bank and invest it, Daddy." The mom asked "Don't you want to buy some new toys?" The child said "No, I have enough toys." I was flabbergasted. It changed my perception of raising children and how you teach them.

If you are an entrepreneur, a taxes category is very helpful to put money aside when taxes are due. You may want to add employees, commissions, contractors, expenses, utilities, advertising, supplies, tools, personal income and a savings category for your business. If we have learned anything from the pandemic, it is to make sure we have enough savings to keep us afloat. Lastly, always keep track of your mileage.

Suppose you don't have a personal computer where you can consistently update and save your sheet, a great alternate option is Google Drive. Open a Google Spreadsheet in your Google Drive, which is free if you have a Gmail address. You can easily access these files if you have a smartphone or tablet. You can also create a basic template on a friend's computer and print it out. Then, you can fill it in with a pencil and make the changes accordingly, or you can download and print a pre-made blank budgeting sheet. I like to highlight the payments that I've made in green and add a column with the date when I made the payment, the form of payment used (so I can reference it in the future), and the confirmation number. If I couldn't make a payment that month, I mark it in red, so I know that I need to make a double payment next month. This will allow you to see your spending habits visually.

If you want to track your spending habits, you can create other categories like food, social, transportation, unexpected expenses, and whatever is relevant in your life. Every time you buy something in those categories, add it to the spreadsheet to track how much money you spend. You can do this at the end of every night or keep a box of receipts, or at the end of the month, you can update it. It's terrific to see what you're spending your money on so you can start controlling bad habits. You may want to start making iced coffee at home versus buying it at a local business or bringing lunch with you because you realize how much money you're spending on food. Taking the subway avoids spending too much money on gas, parking, or Ubers and Lyfts.

I did this manually until I could afford Intuit, QuickBooks, or whatever software you are comfortable with. These programs link to your bank account and keep track of your expenses for you. You can even take a picture of your receipt, and it will scan, save a copy, and categorize it in the software system while adding the amount to your spending for budgeting or tax purposes. The first few months you must categorize each purchase. In the event you purchase from that vendor again, the software automatically organizes it for you, saving so much time preparing for taxes and analyzing spending.

This spreadsheet tactic did not only declutter my home of paper, but it helped me finally stay organized and focused.

This is a long but good story of why you need to keep your confirmation number, canceled check, or money order for any payment to the government. Take a screenshot of the canceled check, money orders or a credit card statement you made the payment with and save it forever. You can skip and go to the next paragraph if you do not want to read it, but it's a good story:

Seventeen years ago, I paid a $10 fine for a ticket I received for hanging out with an idiot who was drinking a beer on the street. I was not drinking, but the police officer didn't care and gave us both tickets. I was 19 years old. I paid the fine with a money order, and I remember this because it was the 1st money order I had ever purchased.

Seventeen years later, I was pulled over while driving, mind you I had been pulled over several times since the incident, but no one ever mentioned anything. I am friends with many police officers, and no one ever said anything when they ran my name. I got pulled over this one time, and they tried to arrest me because, apparently, I had a seventeen-year warrant for this $10 ticket! Luckily (that was GOD), I was with a cop friend that day. I had asked him to accompany me, and he was following me as I was driving someplace. My friend, who has a high-level ranking officer in internal affairs, talked to the cops and assured them I would take care of it.

All I had to do was go into the city and pay the $10 again since I didn't keep the money order after seven years, which is the amount of time I was told you have to save receipts. **But wait!**

After you pay it, you have to go to another department for them to remove it from your record! Even if you paid, it is not removed from your record, and they can still come after you, which is what happened to me. Therefore, you, as a private citizen, need to confirm it is removed! It is not done automatically. It may be done automatically now, but it wasn't then. Even so, it's good to know so you can check and confirm this does not happen to you or someone you know.

I did that, and I have a receipt for both the payment and removal. I scanned the receipt and sent it to multiple email addresses in case I ever need to pull it up in let's say another seventeen years. I am keeping that receipt forever. What I do not understand is, I have changed my driver's license address every time I moved, so they had a record of my addresses. I had been at the previous address for eleven years and this one for thirteen years. Why was I never sent any notifications? Why was I never told this any other time I got a ticket or showed up to court to dismiss a ticket? Why now seventeen years later is this popping up? That's another book I am working on.

Bitcoin & Other Cryptocurrencies

I am not a financial advisor, and the following suggestions should not be taken as financial advice. Please conduct your own research and due diligence before making any decisions, Cryptocurrencies are volatile and should be considered a gamble. Contact a professional before implementing anything suggested in these pages.

I learned many fascinating things about bitcoin and other Cryptocurrencies. You can buy bitcoin and other

Cryptocurrencies from Coinbase, Cash App, KuCoin, Binance, and other exchanges. Each exchange carries various Cryptocurrencies, which I will refer to as Crypto's. After purchasing Crypto's, any currencies you do not plan to sell for a while should be transferred to an independent wallet to store them in. There are hot wallets (online / app wallets), and cold wallets referred to as hard wallets - small electronic external devices that hold your Crypto and communicate with exchanges when you need to sell them.

If you have the Cash app on your phone, you can link it to your bank account and then buy bitcoin. If you prefer to dabble in other Crypto's like XRP Ripple, XLM Stellar Lumens, DOGE Doge Coin, or VET Vechain, you need to sign up for an exchange. Most exchanges will ask you to verify your identity before buying Crypto with your credit card or initialing a withdrawal from the exchange. They call this a KYC Verification. The verification usually involves you sending a picture of your driver's license front and back, and sometimes a selfie of you holding your driver's license. Other exchanges may require your passport information. Each exchange carries various Cryptos but not all exchanges carry every Crypto. You may need to sign up for several exchanges to acquire the Cryptocurrencies you seek.

In the recent past, Bitcoin has doubled every four years (roughly three years and nine months), so it's predicted to double in the next one to two years. This is due to what is referred to as halving, which is when what miners earn is split in half, and many miners sell their bitcoin to take their profits, and the market rises for a year or two and then drops. As of 2021, with the entry of institutions buying bitcoin, the rhythm of the market has changed drastically. There will still be a halving of bitcoin for the miners. However, it may be difficult to predict if that will affect the price, if the current purchases are retained by these institutions and not sold or dumped.

I started investing in 2020 with $1000 by January 2021, it turned into $4500. I cashed out my initial investment and learned how to invest in Crypto with the remainder. Some people buy and hold, and others trade it like the stock market as some exchanges like KuCoin allow you to have limits and margin accounts. I decided to get into Crypto as I needed a slingshot move, a moment that will propel me forward financially to make up for the years I spent traveling and enjoying my life.

It's a volatile fluctuating market, so consider it a gamble. There are no guarantees. I believe the people that grow it and take it out before the market crashes win. It's a gamble like the stock market. If Bitcoin isn't your thing, look up other Cryptocurrencies. Rumor has it, banks, the medical field, and even Amazon are investing in releasing their own Cryptocurrencies.

If you are wondering how to get started on Bitcoin, the easiest way is to sign up for Coinbase or Cash App.
This is how to buy Bitcoin if you have Cash App:

1. It's simple. You download the Cash app.
2. Link it to your bank account.
3. You click on your face icon on the upper left.
4. You click on bitcoin.
5. You click on buy bitcoin.
6. Enter the amount you want to buy, and voila, it is converted into bitcoin. You can then transfer it to a Crypto wallet or an exchange.

If you are not looking to exchange your bitcoin, you should put it in a bitcoin or Crypto wallet, which I'm still learning about. I've heard people put their money in these wallets and forget the password and have lost millions. Others die without leaving the info to anyone, and that money is lost. Keep that in mind. Make sure you leave detailed instructions if you plan on leaving them to your family in the event of a mishap.

There are hard wallets that look like USB memory sticks where you can load your Crypto onto. These wallets need to be secured in a safe place. When you want to exchange your Crypto, you can connect to your phone or desktop and upload your Crypto to an exchange and initiate the trade that you desire. When your transaction is complete you can cash out to your bank or transfer the remaining and/or new Crypto back to your wallet. If you lose your hard wallet, you have essentially lost your Crypto.

There are also soft wallets that are software-based apps that can be accessed and stored on your desktop or phone. They essentially work the same as a hard wallet. However, soft wallets are more susceptible to hackers who may gain access to your computer or phone.

What I did that helped me tremendously is I made a spreadsheet of every transaction. I entered the name of the coin and the contract address I bought it with, so I could compare it to any other migrations or to see if it was a scam. I kept track of the price I bought it at, the number of coins/tokens to see (like if it's growing for the ones that reward you every time there's a tax).

Then, I added a column, where if it migrates, I can add the new contract address and the date. Everything is always dated. If you have a lot of coins, this method helps you keep track of them and aids in checking on them. I check every two months to see if there's any migrations. After losing a substantial amount to migrations, I missed. May my loss be your lesson.

I was overseas in Peru filming in the jungle for my documentary The Indigenous Documentary (www.theindigenousdocumentary.com). It is an ongoing project as the goal is to visit all 6 continents. Monetary gifts are accepted in case anyone wants to contribute.

I am currently in a Crypto black hole, where I dedicate myself to watching four to eight hours of YouTube videos to learn about sleeping giants which are Crypto's that are about to blow up, Crypto vocabulary, and anything else I don't know yet. It is a fascinating world.

Car Insurance

As noted in the beginning of this book, I was in a car accident. I want to teach people everything I didn't know. I will be speaking about my experience, but this could easily be replaced by any other victim of an accident.

Please make sure you have good coverage. You never know when you will be in an accident. If the collision causes damage to another's body, you will need sufficient coverage to cover their medical expenses. No one expects to get into an accident. Still, when it happens, if you get hurt, it's difficult to recoup from it, mentally, physically, financially, and emotionally, but that's another book.

No-Fault Coverage: If you ever get into a car accident and feel any type of pain within the first three days, get a lawyer immediately, then go to the emergency room to document that pain. Your lawyer should be able to guide you from there. You have **thirty days** to file a no-fault application to access the no-fault coverage. If you do not file within that timeframe you will not be covered by no-fault. I recommend getting a lawyer immediately if you were not at fault, if it was a significant impact or some part of your body hurts or aches.

Every state is different, and the laws are constantly changing, but in New York State, you must have $50,000 of no-fault coverage. What that means is that when you get into an accident, if you need to see a doctor, call an ambulance, go to the emergency room, have surgery, or get physical therapy, you have up to $50,000 in medical expenses.

You can pick and choose whichever doctor you prefer to go to. I suggest thoroughly researching doctors if surgery is required. When you call a doctor, ask if they accept no-fault coverage because not all doctors take that. There is a special no-fault rate that they must abide by. If you have Medicaid, they must use that as their rates, which are usually much lower, and you have a more comprehensive range of doctors to choose from. You can also use your health insurance if you have a plan. After No-fault is exhausted, some companies will work with you on a lien; others won't. If your physical therapy office won't, it's difficult for a new office to take you on a lien so make sure the physical therapy office you initially go to will continue therapy on a lien if no-fault runs out. Also, check their rates as some people charge way too much.

I never knew about this when the accident happened. When they asked me if anything was wrong or needed an ambulance, I said no because I didn't want to pay for an ambulance, which I knew was very expensive, usually over $1000. They tried to tow my car, and they said I would have to pay for the tow then get reimbursed. I did not want them to tow my car because I needed it, and I didn't have the money to pay for the tow and then wait to get reimbursed. I didn't understand how any of this worked, but now I know reimbursements take forever to get back (about 30-60 days), so be very careful what you pay for out-of-pocket.

No-fault coverage covers any physical therapy, surgeries, ambulance, emergency hospital visits, miles, or transportation to doctor's visits (not parking), and anything related to the accident. Those expenses must be submitted every 30 days. It also covers reimbursements for lost wages (a percentage of your income up to a certain maximum allowable amount). If you had to stop working, you have to provide two years' worth of taxes. If your taxes are not up to date, you have to file them, and it's going to take forever for you to get reimbursed for lost wages.

Also, know that they have these appointments called IME's (Independent Medical Exam) where you meet the insurance company's doctors, who check you to report their findings. Their goal is to sign off saying you are okay so they can cut off your no-fault. If they find that you are okay, when clearly you are not, the no-fault gets cut off, and you have to work off of liens, loans, your private health insurance company, pay out of pocket, or live with the pain.

Lost Wages: Keep in mind, if you're an independent contractor, you only get reimbursed based on the net amount, not the gross amount. That is the amount left after you deduct your expenses. Even though your expenses may include part of your car insurance, mobile service, or utilities, these are still costs you still incur, whether you're working or not. According to the courts, those expenses are disregarded; they calculate it based on the net amount you take home as personal pay. You get 80% of that amount (in NY). I received about $186 a week, which is below the poverty line, that doesn't even cover my rent and utilities, let alone food and car insurance. I made that working two to three hours. I did not work 40 hours a week, I worked maybe 20 hours or less since I was paid per project. I made more money per project than if I were paid per hour.

Imagine how I felt when I had to pay rent, a cell phone bill that was $120 a month, cable TV and Wi-Fi, which I need to work that cost $230 a month. I've since cut off cable TV and only use WiFi to utilize a Roku, and I bought an antenna to access local TV stations which cost like $10-$20 on Amazon. If you choose to buy an antenna, make sure it has the right connection. Check to see if you have HDMI, coaxial, or RCA - those three cords that are red, yellow, and white, the one you choose should fit one of the connectors on the back of your TV. My car insurance was $267 a month. Yeah, I'm in New

York, so everything is more expensive for one car. Now, it's close to $400 a month, and I was only getting $184 a week, a total of $4300 for eight months.

When I received the money for lost wages, I would only be living off of $736 a month, which is way below the poverty line. This barely covered ¼ of my monthly expenses. At this point, you can get food stamps, Medicaid, and probably some other services, but I didn't because I physically couldn't stand in line or get there. I didn't have money to pay for parking, and I couldn't take the bus or train because I couldn't walk for more than a few minutes or go up and down multiple stairs. It was ridiculous and unfair, and it made me so angry I had to find different ways of surviving. Ergo, this book. Thank you for purchasing it.

Things to think about:

We need to change the laws so an independent contractor receives 80% of their full weekly pay (regardless of deductions because you still have to pay some of the recurring expenses). Since we are mandated to pay car insurance, it should cover everything when we need it. Think about all the people who have never been in an accident and paid insurance their entire lives. Where does that money go? They go to corporate bonuses, holiday parties, and daily breakfast for the staff. What about the people that are in major accidents that need to be covered? They have to fight the insurance company to get the money they need to cover their injuries and losses. There should never be a fight. I was not fully covered. Therefore, I did not fully recover.

I still have nerve damage that shows up in various ways, and I have to go to the emergency room every few months for pain. Do not settle until you know how this can affect you long term. I'm just one of how many?

Keep in mind they make interest off the money that is in the insurance company bank accounts, so they have a surplus of funds. Collecting on an insurance claim should not be this difficult or dissuasive.

Loans: It's safe to say I didn't have enough money to pay my monthly expenses, so I had to take out loans. When you have a lawsuit, there are companies, which sometimes the lawyers own, who will loan you money based on your case's predicted outcome. They are usually at VERY HIGH interest rates. The loan I had was calculated, so the base amount doubles in two years, which is sometimes how long it takes for a case to settle. So, please note that when you get that settlement check, the lawyers will take their cut first, then the loan amount + the interest to pay the loan company + any outstanding liens + any medical liens you may have accrued through your treatment during the lawsuit. If you take a loan out, be grateful if you see anything after all the payments are made. You can feel happy knowing your pain and suffering are lining everyone's pockets but yours.

The whole point of insurance is to get you closer to being as whole as you were before the accident, not only financially but physically. When Insurance companies fail to do that, a lawsuit ensues. The sad part is they would rather pay their lawyers and doctors to try to find ways to pay you less than to make sure you, the victim, are okay. If they just gave you the money, they pay their lawyers and doctors. There would be no reason to sue.

Instead, they would rather take the insurance money to pay their "colleagues" than the victim. I propose they continue paying your medical expenses after the no-fault rate is exhausted. If you need it, clearly there is a problem if you have exhausted no fault.

The Ramifications: The next few paragraphs are examples that create a similar pattern that many people after an accident experience and insurance companies, juries, arbitrators, and lawyers do not really take into consideration. I am sharing my experience, which again could be used to replace another victim's experience.

I am permanently altered with back, knee, ankle pain, and altered brain function that I should not be experiencing at all had the insurance company covered my medical expenses to get me back to whole - which is the term they use. Had the accident never occurred, I would be a normally functioning 40-year-old. Not only were eight months of recovery stolen from my regular life and daily routine, I had to suffer through it physically and emotionally. Not only was time taken from me, but I cannot fully enjoy the upcoming years as I would have, had I not been impaired from the accident. I feel like I am in the body of a 60-year-old, not a 40-year-old. They robbed me of 20 years of adventures, experiences, fun, and fantastic sex. The worst part is I don't have any children yet. I can only imagine what carrying a child would be like with the back pain I have to endure already. I'm assuming it would be more difficult and uncomfortable because my body does not work as it did. It was not my fault, and there is nothing I could do about it. Instead of taking care of me, they took care of themselves.

Then, after all that, not only am I in a financial hole that I have to claw my way out of, but I am still not whole physically and unable to work at the same rate, stamina, physical or mental capacity, and vigor as before because of the pain and disabilities. I make more mistakes because the calculations are wrong from the brain damage experienced. I have had to reduce categories, turn down jobs, and cancel some because of the pain. Everything takes way longer and hurts.

The insurance company's solution is to find another line of work. Okay, let's say I could find a profession that pays more, which is highly unlikely, if I went back to administrative work, I couldn't perform at the same level because of the memory loss and altered brain function. Then, there is the pain; it comes and goes, and there are some good days, but more bad days. After an accident, there shouldn't be bad days. No one counts or cares about the bad days you have to deal with on an emotional and physical level. These are days you should have never had to deal with in the first place, but now you do, and it affects every minute of your life, FOREVER, or at least the remainder of your life, technically pain and suffering which they feel you do not deserve to be compensated for. They will try to minimize what the value of that is. Your once happy, joyful life is permanently altered, and mental anguish affects every part of your life. But hey, they got paid.

Also, keep in mind that the pain and brain issues compound over time, causing me to be in more pain and incur difficulties in performing daily tasks way before I should have had I aged naturally. I have extreme difficulty going up and down stairs and am experiencing more knee and ankle pain. The ankle pain is somehow directed to the healing process of the knee. I believe my alignment is off, but we are checking that soon. I was recently pregnant and had a miscarriage, and I am not sure if it's linked to all the pain and stress I was/am experiencing as a result from the accident.

Not to mention, I am unable to participate in activities and excursions that liberate my soul and add value to my life. Some people may say that doesn't matter, but it does, because one accident can change your way of life in a way that creates a domino effect into all aspects of your life, eventually leading to the decline of your happiness and joy, which affects all aspects of your life. They are more bad days than good days, and there should be no bad days. Had the insurance company just done their due diligence and made sure I was physically fine by using the insurance money to cover me, there would be no reason to sue. If a lawsuit is necessary, the insurance company should cover the victim's legal fees as it should have never had to get this far if the insurance company and the person liable for the accident had done what they were supposed to.

Emergency Fund

Saving is so important, and it's not emphasized as much in some homes. I remember I walked into a client's house, and they had a four-year-old son. The dad gave the child $100 in front of me, and the kid said to his dad, "can you put it in the bank so it can grow." This child at four years old grasps and implements the concept. It's lucrative and fundamentally necessary to save enough money to get you through a rough patch.

Suze Orman (look her up) gives excellent financial advice. It is in your best interest to have an emergency fund that covers 2-12 months of income. Eight months is usually recommended, but anything is better than nothing. It's for your protection and mental sanity.

FOOD SHOPPING

I am not a nutritionist, but I will share what I have learned. I realized in my budgeting phases I purchased many items that had a lot of processed ingredients, which included dyes, nitrates, and colors. I was on a strict budget. They were affordable as I had no money, and I didn't read the labels. As I learned, I made more conscious decisions of what I purchased.

In retrospect, I should've just gone to the supermarket and bought lots of fruits and vegetables. I started to buy meat when it's on sale and put it in the freezer, so it wouldn't go bad. I would take fruit before it over ripened and put it in the freezer to make my smoothies.

I learned not to buy anything with a color in the ingredients - red, yellow, blue, etc. Some of those are known to cause cancer. You would have to research to see which ones.

Generally safe food to buy:
Peanuts (unflavored / can be salted)
Dried fruit without added sugar
Dehydrated fruit without added sugar
Nut and Dried Fruit mixes without added sugar
Frozen French fries or potato wedges

Frozen vegetables
Kettle chips or popcorn (4 ingredients or less)
Real cheese made with milk or cultured milk
Plain Greek yogurt (check for added sugar)
Frozen Ravioli

I was taught to stay away from anything that says "drink" - pineapple drink, orange drink, etc. It's pure sugar, flavoring, and chemicals. You're better off just buying lemons/limes, sugar, or honey and making your own lemonade. I suggest purchasing a juicer and buying fruit and making your own juice. When you choose this method, you tend to drink less sugar because your body is getting natural sugar, diminishing the craving for artificial sugar.

Make sure the food you buy has food in it and not flavoring to make it taste like food.

These are suggestions. Don't get me wrong, I love all food. I still buy unhealthy items all the time. I'm not perfect, nor am I trying to be. I have chosen to make a conscious decision to make healthier choices for my body, and I am sharing those with you. I do love me some sour cream and onion Stax potato chips.

Mother's Day Flowers

In NYC, you find stores with flowers outside that sell bouquets for $10. For Mother's Day, I like to buy closed roses a few days before Mother's Day (when they are still $10) and place them in a vase with water; they start to bloom just in time for Mother's Day when they jack up the price!

Life Insurance

If you haven't figured it out, I'm a knowledge seeker, and I love learning and sharing that knowledge. This is only my opinion and what I understand about life insurance. Keep in mind there are various policies with a multitude of varying terms.

Disclaimer: Please confirm anything I write in this section with your agent; this section was created just so that you can get a little bit more information if you did not have it already when you're sitting down with an insurance agent. Knowledge is power and should be shared. The rules, terms, and topics mentioned are subject to change, especially with each presidency who may change the laws. This is just what I understand at this current moment (September 2019).

Whole life: I have two policies. I have a traditional whole life policy with the cash value, then I have a term policy. So how does this work? This is how I understand it for a whole life policy. You have your insurance policy, then you have a cash value. When paying your premium every month, part of the premium (monthly payment) is going towards the policy benefit, which your beneficiaries may collect if you pass. For instance, if you have a $100,000 coverage and the other part goes into a cash value portion (they sometimes call this a savings account), you have to pay that premium until you're 100 years old or you die. That's basically forever. Some premiums are level, which means that they're the same every month, and others are fluctuating; as you age, the monthly premium increases.

If your policy lapses (you miss a payment), you may lose all your coverage, but you can keep the cash value. There is an option you can add into your policy that covers the missed payment with your cash value, but you have to ask for that if they offer that. Some plans automatically include this feature. However, it is best to always confirm.

When you withdraw money from your cash account, it's considered a loan from yourself, and you must pay that back usually with interest. The monthly premium covers that "loan" over time, or you can add additional funds to cover it.

Now, we have recently encountered a pandemic, and I was able to use the cash value to cover my monthly premium payments until I was able to pay them again. The cash value can be very useful. The theory of the cash value is not only to cover you during emergencies. It is generally invested in the stock market, so it can grow and pay your premiums in the future as you age and your premiums increase. Check to make sure the interest you earn is not capped. If it is, at what rate? The market generally yields roughly a 10% return. Some years, there are losses. On the years the market is above your cap, they are pocketing the difference.

Back to paying premiums for the entirety of your life, aka forever, the goal is to get the cash value to equal or be greater than the policy benefit because when you die you don't get both. Yeah, I said it. If the cash value is higher, your family would get that cash value (and the insurance company keeps the benefit). If the policy benefit amount is higher, your family will get that (but then the insurance company then keeps the cash value,) basically paying themselves back, even though you paid your premium. They have been investing and growing both amounts and earning a lot of money off of your monthly payments (unless you die shortly after getting the policy). Generally, you don't get both. There are policies that are structured to use the cash value to cover your policy when you are older, a few do give both the benefit and cash value, but you will pay much higher premiums, and you must request this.

It all depends on the plan you choose and the conversation you have with your agent. They now have updated plans that include long term care coverage when you are older. I don't have that. My plan allowed me to deduct money from my cash value as a loan for emergencies and my interest was capped at 4%. Thankfully, I had this type of policy, and it saved me, because every time I needed money it was there for me during unexpected emergencies. It's still my money and I can always access it, but because of the way it's structured, I have to pay it back with 2% interest. This gets deducted and repaid from the premiums I already pay. Keep in mind because I have taken out so much money over the years, it is unlikely I will have enough to cover my premiums when I get older. I just like the fact that I was able to use the cash value as a savings account / emergency fund.

Term Insurance:

This option focuses on insuring you for a benefit amount for any period of time, up to 35 years this time limit varies per state and depends on the plan you choose. If you outlive the policy and it expires, so does your benefit amount. You lose the policy and the premiums.

With Primerica, their motto is pay less monthly and invest the difference, so your investments take care of you when you are older or pass. They set you up with the term insurance for however many years you choose if you are young, your family gets the benefit amount (policy amount), and they receive your separate independant investments when you die.

A term policy is beneficial because when you're young, if you pass, your partner / family has coverage for large expenses, like your mortgage, educational costs, childcare, monthly income of the missing partner. As you get older and closer to retirement, the house should be paid off or close to it, the kids should all be older, and out of school, so you don't need that much coverage. Term insurance is best if someone passes young and you don't want to keep paying insurance after you retire or until you're 100 years old.

Primerica has something called a fab account where you can put up to $10 a month into it, and if you miss a payment, it will automatically take the money from your fab account so that your policy doesn't lapse. They can do that until you reach $5000. If you need emergency money, you can take it out anytime you want. It's your money, and you do not have to pay it back, nor is there any interest attached to a withdrawal. If you reach the end of your term and are still alive, congratulations!!! They will return the fab balance at the end of your policy. Also, if you are ever in a financial crisis event like the recent pandemic you can use your fab balance to pay your monthly premium so it does not lapse. You must call your provider and let them know how long you would like them to deduct the premium from your fab account balance. You may have to call monthly to ensure it is done, as was my experience.

Bad Experiences: Now, my family has had their share of lousy insurance experiences. So, I'm going to share some more key terms and phrases you should know about when you're purchasing your policy.

When my aunt died, my family had been paying $100 a month for what they thought was a $100,000 policy, only to find out it was an accidental death and dismemberment policy, which meant she had to die in a car accident or be dismembered for my family to get that money. Obviously, she was dying of cancer, so that wasn't an option. So, my family members had been paying all of this money all of this time for nothing. They thought they had an insurance policy that covered her in the event of her death, and that's not what they had. It is essential for you to look at what type of policy you have. If you don't know, ask your insurance agent, or I highly recommend Eileen Mamaril Scheinznach from Primerica (**primerica.com/eileenmamaril**). She genuinely cares about you, checks up on you, and loves educating people. She focuses on term policies and financial services. She is great to contact for setting up an IRA or an IRA rollover.

One more quick educational horror story, my mother had an insurance policy from a prevalent insurance company who shall not be named. The policy was purchased in the 1980s. She prepaid a lot of money into it but moved around a lot, so they had lost her at some point, and she thought the policy was paid up. They are supposed to do their due diligence to contact you, which they didn't. When she moved, she lived in that next house for 11 years, moved again to a house for five years, and moved one final time, she's been in that third house for over ten years. It wasn't until over 25 years later after they depleted all that money she put into it, that they sent her a letter saying she still had a policy.

We contacted the company and were told they had converted her policy from whole life to term because she lapsed with payments, and they used whatever cash value that remained to pay the policy. Apparently, she had enough money left to cover her until she was sixty-five. She was sixty-two at the time; can you imagine how much cash value was there to cover the policy for 25 years? Then, it would be exhausted and canceled. She asked for the cash value that was left, which was about $2000. She could either just let it be and see if she died or take out the money. She took the money. If you get a policy, keep it paid and make sure your address is up to date.

Organza Bags

I know this sounds weird, but organza bags are great for many things. You can get them at the Dollar Tree or any discount store. They are great for a multitude of things. The tiny ones are excellent for that little piece of soap that nobody can ever really use. You can put it in the organza bag and tie it up, and it becomes an exfoliating soap holder. If you get the larger ones and put your bar of soap in there. It's far more affordable than buying loofah sponges.

The larger ones are great for gifts, and the smaller ones are great for loose tea. I'm going through this whole organic loose tea phase, where I buy dried flowers, vegetables, and fruits and boil them. You could use a strainer, which also works, but I like the organza bags.

It's really cute to gift the teas. You can put a bunch of tea in the little bags, maybe like twelve, then put them in a small beautiful gift box and give them out as an artisanal gift with a beautifully written note card. This works exceptionally well if you're on a budget and you have a lot of loose tea and need a gift.

Parking

To date there is one mobile app you can use to pay for parking in NYC called ParkNYC. ParkNYC is an app that allows you to add time up to the maximum designated time permitted by the meter. If you paid for 30 min but need more time and the meter allows for 1 hour you can extend it up to that one hour but not beyond it. After the time has expired you must come down and pay by credit or debit card at the meter. You cannot pay again on the app once the time has expired (They want to try to give you a ticket.) You can pay again via the app after you have paid by card. There must be a break.

I recommend paying with a credit card first, taking a picture of the meter. It's the six-digit number on the side of the meter or on the bottom of the street parking signage, so you have the meter number if you need to pay for parking on the app. Set your alarm, so when your time runs out you can pay for the next hour or two with the app. If you need more time afterwards, you must come down and pay with your card or cash. You cannot pay on the app over and over. There must be a break. That may change in the future as many meters are not recognizing your card when you try to pay.

Here's a tip: In some locations To park for one hour is $3.75, but two hours is $10.50, instead of $7.50, which is what two hours logically would be. So, to save money, pay one hour upfront. Then, pay for one hour with the app and go back down and pay another hour. Do the next hour with the app. Every two hours, you'll save $3, which adds up. Sometimes time is more important than money, and its best to max it out, but if you need to save money, you can do so. If you will be anywhere for a full day, it might be more cost effective to pay for parking at a parking garage.

Early Bird Parking Specials

Many parking garages have specials before 8-10 AM where the price is significantly lower than if you come in after that time. You would have to check with each garage independently and find out when their early bird pricing starts and what it would be. If there is an early bird special, it might be a better idea to try to get your client or the person you're visiting to allow you to come earlier, or to just arrive earlier for the early bird parking. Then, sit at a café, have some coffee, and relax for an hour or two before your job starts. It's also a great opportunity for you to surf the web or work via WIFI while you wait. In some cases, the savings are significant and worth taking advantage of.

.

Product Insurance

Always buy the insurance when you buy a stick or cordless vacuum cleaner. It will always die or lose suction within a year or two. With insurance, you'll just get a replacement or get your money back. I insure everything.

I recommend always buying the accidental and water damage insurance for three years, if applicable, on a laptop or any electronics that costs over $100. Again, if anything happens, they fix it for you, replace it, or give you your money back. Don't risk it. You can purchase the insurance on websites like QVC, Walmart, Amazon, eBay, or Best Buy at the time of purchase, or you can go to www.squaretrade.com and insure it independently. All you need to do is buy the insurance, upload your receipt, and you are done. If you need to make a claim, log on or call them and make a claim.

The Curse of the Overdraft Fees

This really affected me the most as a young adult - banking systems overdraft fees: If you do not feel like reading this, just skip to the end of this section to prepaid gift card balances. No matter how much money I put in the bank, I was always negative from the insufficient fund's fees, which kept accruing. Side note: We need to fix this as a country because it's just ridiculous. $35 for any overdraft charge is egregious. You can have overdrafts that total less than $10 each and be charged $35 each (I believe it's legally up to three a day unless this presidency changes that too), so $105 for less than $50 of charges.

Some banks have algorithms that split your charges to get the most overdrafts. Real-time banking would avoid this - deduct the money the moment the charge is made would let us know how much money is really available, and then people would be less likely to get an overdraft. Instead, they claim, they post items when the merchant claims the funds which conveniently causes an overdraft fees.

Also, when someone deposits a check, once it clears, the amount should be backdated, as a check should be viewed as a cash deposit. The bank's service/duty is to clear the check. So this policy of charging insufficient funds while a check is clearing because the bank chooses to extend a hold on a check or it takes longer to clear is appalling. For example, Chase Manhattan Bank said, and I quote, "Well, the funds did not clear when the transaction was posted, so you incurred insufficient charges for each transaction that was deemed an overdraft." Banks charge you insufficient funds fees even though the money is there and **shows up on your current**

balance, but you're still considered negative because the funds haven't been cleared in their system.

You can have screenshots of your running balance with it stating that you have a positive cash flow because it "seems" like the check is being accounted for. You see the amount in the bank, less each transaction that is pending or is coming in, and the final cash flow seems positive. All the while, the deposit says pending for days, yet it shows in your running balance you have more than enough money. Then when it clears suddenly everything changes and you have all these overdraft fees and insufficient funds fees, backdated because miraculously, the check still had not officially cleared within their system. Then why did you make it seem like I was in a positive cash flow and the check was covering these costs. How can you legally show one thing and then suddenly change it.

I have screenshots to prove what I am seeing. There is more, get this, sometimes they choose to extend the hold so they can legally charge you multiple days of insufficient funds fees, and this is perfectly legal. In a world full of technology, I cannot understand how a bank cannot clear funds within minutes when they can process pin code debit purchases in real-time. Why would they use such deceptive tactics? Oh yeah, because they want to rip your hard-earned money out of your hands, like the police do with the camera tickets. They need to fund their salaries like the insurance companies do when they don't want to pay for your recovery in a car accident, but they can pay lawyers and their doctors to minimize the severity of your pain in their reports so you get less money.

The crazy thing is sometimes they will clear $100 the day of the deposit, and sometimes they don't. It's at their discretion if they choose to, there is no consistency. Then they say, "our system won't let us give you more than one refund as a courtesy." What do you mean the system doesn't allow it?

These loopholes need to stop. The money was deposited, and it was the bank's fault for taking their time to clear it. We live in such a technologically advanced time where you can Zelle money instantly, yet the bank cannot clear a check electronically. Get it together. If they have to extend a hold, the amount should cover all purchases made from the deposit date once the check clears. Please note this has been my personal experience, and this is what they explained to me. They are just soooo wrong on so many levels, especially ethically.

Anyway, there should be a scale for overdraft fees, $5-$15 is a reasonable amount, but $35 is ridiculous. I don't believe the insufficient funds fee should be more than the actual transaction, but that's another book. If anyone in banking, finance, or any banking representative is reading this, you may want to consider making some changes.

PRE-PAID GIFT CARD BALANCES

If you have a low balance on a gift card like Starbucks, CVS, Walmart, Ladurée, etc., sometimes you can add more money to the card and keep it on the side for emergencies (when you are low on funds). Other times they will use the balance of the card on your next purchase and then charge you the difference, do not throw away a card because there are a few dollars left.

However, for prepaid cash cards like Visa, MasterCard, American Express, or Discover, if you have a really low cash balance, you can refill your balance on your Starbucks, Dunkin Donuts, iTunes, Amazon cards, and more. What you do is use that balance on the card to replenish your account, so you don't lose it. For example, if there is $2.11 on a prepaid cash gift card, you can log onto the website of choice. On Amazon. there is a gift card section where you can reload your gift card, which is your credit balance on Amazon. Click Reload my gift card balance, enter $2.11, then the card number, expiration date, and sometimes pin, and it will transfer the amount to the Amazon account. The next time you purchase something on Amazon, they will use the gift card balance first, then charge you the difference. Regardless of the amount on your card, you won't lose it.

Real Estate

Buy whatever you can get your hands on. Go to auctions, look for foreclosures, fix it up, rent, or sell. Homes are far more affordable outside of the city.

Air B&B has been a huge source of income for many people. I met a guy about three years ago who I sold a surfboard to for a friend. This guy came to pick up the surfboard, and I ended up driving him to the beach because his conversation was so compelling. I learned he was a musician and had a five-bedroom apartment in Harlem. One room was his music studio. When his roommate moved out, they Air B&B'd it for $100 a night. They rented it for 20 days, which was $2000. The next roommate moved out, and they Air B&B'd that room they were averaging $4000 a month in extra income.

He gave up his studio and Air B&B'd that room, and they were pulling in $6000 a month, which paid the rent and gave them extra income. They rented another five-bedroom apartment in the building, and one of them moved into that one. They rented four rooms in that apartment. They were pulling in $16k a month before they deducted rent and electricity. They probably took home about $10,000, so $5,000 a month each in profit. They could write off the rent, wifi, and expenses like coffee, tea and snacks they provided for their guests. Then, they bought a house in Brooklyn and turned it into eight bedrooms that they rent for $50 a night. pulling in about $8000-$12,000 at full capacity, which more than covers the mortgage, water, electricity, and heat. They are real estate owners now, and their life path pivoted drastically.

God only knows how many other investments and ventures they are up to now. The laws are changing rapidly to hinder these types of rentals.

Savings (Roth IRA, IRA, and Money Market Accounts)

Disclaimer: I am not a financial planner. I am sharing what I have heard and learned; please check with your financial planner or get one to confirm accuracy.

This is what I was told to do, and I'm sharing it with you. Any invested money in the market is a gamble.

These accounts fluctuate with the stock market. Generally, the stock market has grown an average of about 10 percent per year over the years. Some years are good, and others are not. The benefit of the market is compound interest. You get in, invest, and do not touch it, even if it crashes, it tends to bounce back. The longer your money is in the market, the more it grows. People in their early twenties benefit from putting just $25 a week. I suggest more if you are capable, and in forty years, that could grow to be more or less $1 million with compounded interest (look it up). It sounds like a lot but with inflation that amount will not stretch as far as it does now.

Roth IRA: Go to your bank, tell them you want to open up a Roth IRA and you want $25 (or whatever you can afford) deducted every week into your account. Then you want to invest that money in index mutual funds. If you don't request it to be invested, it just sits there like a savings account. It will not grow.

Now, keep in mind if you lose your job, you need to go to your bank and tell them to stop the withdrawals. I don't want you to have to suffer the way that I did with insufficient fees (refer to the about me section if you skipped that earlier).

Below are two random pieces of knowledge that were shared with me that I believe are worth sharing:

1. I heard from someone or a movie (not sure if this is true, but It's a good story). Warren Buffett (billionaire) has been driving the same car for 30 years. He's worth seventy billion. He says he would never buy or lease a vehicle because that $350 a month he would be spending if you invested in the stock market in three to five years can make you $1 million. You might want to think about taking $350 a month and putting it away in the stock market or your IRA. He self directs his money market accounts. This is hearsay, I am not sure how accurate this is, but you get the idea.

2. Someone told me once that if you live with your parents, you should take the money that you would've spent on rent, which would've been like - let's say $1200 for a studio (this is NY). Since your living with your parents, you could take ½ ($600) or ¼ ($150) and give that to your parents as rent and the other ½ ($600) that you're supposed to be paying in rent, had you moved out, you put into a separate savings account, IRA, money market account or upcoming as a down payment for a house or apartment. That math breaks down to 600×12 months is $7200. You can have a down payment for a house or an apartment in three years. That is something you might want to think about. If you are a private person, you can do this, and no one has to know.

Stocks

Etrade - I suggest opening an Etrade account and depositing money in there periodically so that when you get a good stock tip, there is money in there to buy. All I know is if you were investing in 2020-2021 CBD, Marijuana, Tech, and Healthcare were a good bet. Now it's AI. If you want to know which ones specifically, I suggest you contact your financial advisor. If you don't have one, get one or get rich friends who may throw you a tip every now and then.

Cash App - I just learned Cash App allows you to buy portions of stock and purchase stock immediately! If you cannot afford one stock of Amazon, which is currently about $2500, you can pay as much as you can afford. Perhaps you only have $100 or $5, you can log onto the cash app, hit the stock icon on the bottom of the screen, and enter the word Amazon (or the stock of your choice). The stock code for Amazon should pop up. Confirm it is the correct code. You can do this with any business. Once confirmed, click the buy option, enter the amount you can invest, enter your passcode, and voila, you have a portion of the stock that grows at the same percentage rate of owning one stock, if the stock goes up 5%, your portion grows 5%. You can also sell your stocks on the app. They charge a purchase and sell fee, so you may want to look up other apps like Robinhood to compare rates. A little goes a long way. There is no excuse not to invest in stocks any longer. (This was written before that whole Gamestop debacle.)

Unclaimed Funds

Many states have an unclaimed funds department that hold all funds that have not been claimed by the recipient. These could be security deposits you left for services, inheritances, or judgements owed to you. You can look up unclaimed funds in your state and enter your name. You may see several names pop up with a variety of middle initials or addresses. Find the name and address which correspond to you and your address or previous address. They will show you the account. If it is something you recognize, you then enter your information as proof that you are whom you claim to be, along with your new mailing address, and they will send you a check for that amount. Many people have unclaimed funds they are unaware of.

CHAPTER *Eleven*

I'M OUT

That concludes what I have to share with you about thriving on a budget. If you would like to see any updates, check out my website **NYonaBudget.com** and my Facebook page **www.facebook.com/nyoab** that posts free or inexpensive events and deals in the NYC area.

Lastly, I would greatly appreciate any support for a multi-series documentary I am in the process of filming called The Indigenous Documentary, where I visit indigenous tribes and descendants of ancient tribes and document their version of the history of the world, how they heal the body, mind, and spirit, how they use music, how climate change has impacted them, and how corporations removing the natural resources has affected them. Lastly, I would ask them what their message to the world is.

I am incredibly passionate about this project and am looking for funding to cover travel expenses, equipment, donations to tribes, a camera person/assistant, my costs while abroad, editing, and anything else that comes up that I am unaware I would need. If you would like to volunteer services like film editing or audio engineering, I will gladly accept those as well. You can reach me at theindigenousdocumentary@gmail.com

Please check out the website

www.theindigenousdocumentary.com.

Monetary/physical donations and sponsors are welcome, such as camera equipment, airline miles that can be used to travel and visit various tribes, an airline buddy pass, super lightweight camping gear, hotel stays / air b&b's, a place to stay when visiting foreign places, introductions / connections to indigenous tribes, a camera assistant and monetary donations to cover our expenses at home as we travel and embark on this crazy fabulous journey.

The universe implanted this quest in my soul, and I believe I was meant to do this. I have traveled to 24+ countries for work and personal interests, and now I would like to travel for knowledge.

I am in the process of becoming a holistic healer, studying Reiki, crystal, and sound healing, and this quest will not only educate the world but aid me in the calling I have been given by learning from the masters directly. After the documentary, I would like to open a holistic center to heal individuals from the inside out, body, mind, and spirit. Thank you for taking the time to read this, and I look forward to sharing my journey with you. I will also be blogging about the above experiences at www.theindigenousdocumentary.com and on my YouTube channel.

I know you're probably wondering how I do all of this. It's a belief I speak about as a motivational speaker. Stop limiting yourself because society, friends, or family doubt your ability to accomplish something. If that thought, idea, or gift entered your mind / life, it has been given to you because the universe and God believe you can achieve it. Not your friends, not your family, not your coworkers, YOU! You were given that gift; you were given that idea, you were given that belief, so only you can do it. Keep in mind, if you don't do it, the universe will give that to someone else because its goal is to complete its plan, but that's another book.

We are limitless creatures, and if we work together as a tribe and community, we can achieve so much. Do not let anybody divide and conquer you or your dreams. Remember one thing, you cannot do it alone, you need a tribe, you need a squad, you need a team, you need allies because where there are two, you can multiply exponentially.

Thank you for reading my book. XOXO
(mic drop)

ACKNOWLEDGMENTS

First, I need to acknowledge my mother - my rock, my heart, my everything. Thank you for showing me the finer things in life and introducing me to influential individuals. Thank you for bringing me with you to galas, fundraisers and being the perfect example of a lady.

My mom not only raised and nurtured me, but she taught me to never give up. The most memorable thing she shared, "If they can do it, you can do it," and I did, which is why I have achieved so much in this lifetime. Anytime I asked for permission to do something, she always said, "Go, do it. You only live once. You never know who you are going to meet." Mind you, this is 25 years ago before yolo ever existed. Her encouragement and life lessons changed my life and made me who I am.

I sincerely cannot find the words to express how grateful I am for everything she has taught and provided for me. She is a go-getter, a doer, and a beacon of light. Impossible does not exist in her vocabulary. She is and will always be my favorite person on earth. She is why I believe I can accomplish anything and the reason I do.

I must also acknowledge my grandmother, My Tia Carmen, Tia Josephina, Tia Leticia, and Aunt Carmen (My mom's best friend) for teaching me compassion, grace, etiquette, empathy, a joyful/playful manner, forgiveness, and unconditional love.

My grandfather taught me respect, discipline, honor, how to save and be frugal (the emphasis of this book). He taught me to share and make sure everyone is included and taken care of. My grandmother taught me patience, to enjoy and appreciate the little things, and how sitting in comfortable silence with someone you love is priceless.

In addition, I would like to acknowledge my Tio Dino for stepping in as a father figure. He gave me my first two cars and was always there. He taught me Greek and exposed me to the Mediterranean culture and history, which opened my eyes to the world in a different way. He also had a boat and would take us out of Port Jefferson, NY, on fishing trips, which has nurtured my sea-bearing legs. Thank you for so many unique life experiences.

I must also thank my Uncle Boris. He loved me very much. He was also a father figure in my life and always made sure I was provided for. I would also like to thank Rosetta, Concetta, Francis, and Vito, friends who welcomed me into their home and family. They exposed me to Italian culture and helped raise me.

The culmination of the life lessons I received from my family/framily paired with common sense, and the evolution of technology led to me finding modern ways to live the luxurious life I was exposed to in a very frugal way. Thank you all.

Thank you, Derrek S. Luke for helping me with the initial edit of this book. Derrek is a music songwriter, singer, actor, IT specialist. We have been friends since our junior year of high school when we earned a coveted spot in the COAP (Career Opportunities in the Accounting Profession) program sponsored by Pace University. The program can be found at https://www.nysscpa.org/nextgen/high-school-students/coap.

We spent two weeks dorming at their Westchester location and learned about career opportunities in the accounting profession, business ethics, etiquette, and more. It's too complicated to explain so we tell people we met at accounting camp.

God really does put angels in your path. My very dear friend, Latiqua Williams, whom I met in 2015, at a three-day seminar called WE NYC (Women Entrepreneurs NYC - https://we.nyc) hosted by the New York Women's Chamber of Commerce. We have been friends ever since. When we met, she was writing and has since self-published a book called, **She Did Single Parenting in Heels,** available on **Amazon.com**. Because she did it, I knew I could.

Thank you all for reading this book until the end.

And last but not least thank you God.

Made in the USA
Monee, IL
05 November 2026

67845288R00089